A Transforming Vision

The multi-faceted Word of God never ceases to amaze in its ability to give wisdom and understanding; the Lord's Prayer is no exception. It has always been an important part of the tapestry of a walk with God, yet Dr. William Edgar has opened up new and life changing dimensions of this familiar passage. Approaching this prayer as an "apologetic for the biblical worldview" puts this book in a class by itself. Without a doubt, *A Transforming Vision* will prove to be a pivotal and treasured book in the life of the church.

CARL ELLIS JR.,
Assistant Professor of Practical Theology, Redeemer Seminary, Dallas, Texas

Bill Edgar's *A Transforming Vision* unpacks the Lord's Prayer in order to teach you your faith and change how you pray. To pray is to honestly ask God for something. So say what you mean, and mean what you say. What you ask should be meaning-ful—thoughtful prayer knows who it is talking to and what it is talking about. And you should mean it when you ask—heart-felt prayer feels the weight of true necessities. Most of us drift, because we aren't seeing clearly. Our thoughtful words come out sounding dull. Our fervent words pour forth sounding confused. Or our prayers stumble on sounding both dull and confused! *A Transforming Vision* aims to fill your prayers with the riches of Scripture, so that you will know what you are ask-ing and you will really ask.

DAVID POWLISON,
CCEF Executive Director, Senior Editor, Journal of Biblical Counseling

A Transforming Vision

The Lord's Prayer
as a Lens for Life

William Edgar

William Edgar is Professor of Apologetics at Westminister Theological Seminary in Philadelphia, and an accomplished jazz pianist. He is married to Barbara and they have two children, William and Deborah.

paperback ISBN 978-1-78191-369-7
epub ISBN 978-1-78191-407-6
mobi ISBN 978-1-78191-408-3

First published in 2014
by
Christian Focus Publications Ltd,
Geanies House, Fearn, Ross-shire
IV20 1TW, Scotland
www.christianfocus.com

Cover designed by Daniel van Straaten
Printed by Bell and Bain, Glasgow

MIX
Paper from
responsible sources
FSC
www.fsc.org FSC® C007785

Contents

Preface   7

Introduction   9

1 Why Pray at All?   15

2 The Setting for the Lord's Prayer   37

3 Prayer and the Coming Kingdom   51

4 Our Father Who Art in Heaven,
   Hallowed Be Thy Name   69

5 Thy Kingdom Come, Thy Will Be Done,
   on Earth as It Is in Heaven   89

6 Give Us this Day Our Daily Bread   115

7 And Forgive Us Our Debts
   as We Forgive Our Debtors   141

8 Lead Us not into Temptation
   but Deliver Us from Evil   165

9 For Thine Is the Kingdom and the Power
   and the Glory, Forever and Ever, Amen   185

To

Debbie and Mark

'A threefold cord is not quickly broken'

Preface

To those, including myself, who object: one more book on the Lord's Prayer! I answer, these words have been analyzed and upheld by so many because they are capable of it, and worthy of it. In any age, but particularly our own, this treasure of a prayer is urgently needed. As Augustine once said about praying properly, 'Whatever be the other words we may prefer to say (words which the one praying chooses so that his disposition may become clearer to himself or which he simply adopts so that his disposition may be intensified), we say nothing that is not contained in the Lord's Prayer, provided of course we are praying in a correct and proper way.'

It is my conviction that not only are our prayers not proper if we pronounce words that are not implicitly contained in the Lord's Prayer, but neither are any words in our vocabulary. Thus, the Lord's Prayer is far more than a succinct set of petitions. It represents a world and life view. Although I am not a very good nor consistent praying person, in meditating on the words our Lord taught us, it has dawned on me that they are more than a handy formula for effective praying, which they are, but they are a way of life. The discipline I have taught for some forty five years is Christian Apologetics. This field is about defending and commending the Christian faith. I can think of no better defense or commendation than the Lord's Prayer. Thus, the present volume is intended to frame the prayer as an apologetic for the truth and vitality of the biblical outlook for our times. That is why it is a truth that transforms.

No such project is ever accomplished alone. Along the way I have been encouraged by many people. First, those stalwarts who have written or spoken on the prayer. They range from the church fathers to the sages of our own time. A few of their books are classics. I have referred to them throughout. Second, thanks go to my church, the Lansdale Presbyterian Church, where we say the prayer every Lord's Day. It becomes clear, Sunday after Sunday, that the words are profoundly appropriate for the life of a congregation. That we say Our Father and not just My Father is but one indication of the connection of the prayer to corporate life. As always, I would like to thank my family, especially my wife, Barbara, not only for her encouragement but for being my primary and favorite praying partner. I must also thank Westminster Theological Seminary for providing circumstances favorable to the kind of concentrated meditation required for such a writing project. Finally, my gratitude goes to the excellent editors at Christian Focus Publications. They have greatly improved the text. Any remaining errors or insufficiencies are entirely my own responsibility.

May this book be an encouragement to many who are looking to do justice, to love kindness, and to walk humbly with their God.

William Edgar
Westminster Theological Seminary
2014

Introduction

An Apologetic
for the Biblical World and Life View

We owe to the *Pater Noster*, answered Raphaël, our arts, our monuments, perhaps our sciences, and, greater benefits still! Our modern governments, in which a vast and fruitful society is marvelously represented by five hundred minds, where opposite forces neutralize one another and leaves all the power to civilization. In the face of so many accomplished works, atheism is like a skeleton incapable of begetting. What do you think?

(Balzac, La peau de chagrin)

Too familiar to be familiar

Depending on your culture, or how you were brought up, you may know every melody of *Messiah* by Handel. Perhaps you are more familiar with folk and popular music. You may know by heart the tune and words of *Candle in the Wind* by Elton John, or perhaps *I Still Haven't Found What I'm Looking for* by U2. The irony here is that these songs are magnificent, but we have listened to them so many times, we don't quite hear them anymore. They are like great mountains which you remember from having been there, and perhaps see in a picture book, but you don't climb them anymore, so you don't really know them. Our family used to live in Aix-en-Provence, in the South of France. Although it is a typical town with a rich history, and layers of architecture going back to the Etruscans, and then the Romans, the Enlightenment and the present, one part doesn't seem to fit. The strange granite mountain, *La Sainte Victoire*, simply juts out of nowhere and dominates most of the city and its environs. Even if you have not seen it in person, you will have encountered it in the scores of paintings Paul Cézanne devoted to it. It has become an icon. The reality of it, when you do climb it or walk around its paths, is quite surprising, even bewildering. Yet somehow locals rarely acknowledge it.

The same is true of a masterpiece such as the *Mona Lisa* by Leonardo. Her smile, the folded hands, the imaginary landscape, the light, these are imprinted in our minds. This portrait appears in every art book, and is often caricatured by cartoonists. Modern artists, such as Salvador Dali and Marcel Duchamp reproduced a distorted *Mona Lisa* as an act of rebellion against the Renaissance tradition. If you have ventured into the Louvre, you will discover that the *Mona Lisa* is the most popular attraction in the museum. If you were able to get close enough, battling the crowds, you may have been surprised at its small size and the bullet-proof glass obscuring the pure colors. But even then, did you really see it, or did you simply view it? Why is this painting considered the very apex of art by the world over? Does it deserve its iconic status? A friend of mine, an artist and art historian, decided to put the folklore to the test. Well before the days of high security, he took a small seat, went into the Louvre, and gazed at Lisa del Giocondo, the presumed subject of the painting, for an entire day. At the end, he reported to me, that, yes, once you get past the legend, once you try to actually see the painting and study its every contour, it is truly one of the greatest masterpieces ever conceived. In fact, he told me, a day was not nearly long enough!

The *Lord's Prayer* suffers the same fate. We say it so often, and hear it at services, and so it has become an icon. The minister begins, 'And now, as our Lord has taught us, we are bold to say... Our Father, which art in heaven...' and on to automatic pilot. Even people who are not believers know this prayer by heart. But do they really know it? Do believers really know it? Do we really pray it, or do we just say it?

Perhaps the only time we stop to think about what we are actually saying in the prayer is when we are jolted by one of its phrases, said differently from what we are used to. For example, those from the tradition that asks, 'forgive us our trespasses, as we forgive those who trespass against us,' find themselves surprised, or even offended, when they hear the words, from another tradition, 'forgive us our debts, as we forgive our debtors.' When this happens they somehow feel that this is not the real *Lord's Prayer*.[1] Many have grown up finishing the prayer with, 'For thine is the kingdom, and the power and the glory, forever.' (Some traditions say, 'forever and ever.' It can be jarring to hear it differently.) Some liturgies leave this phrase out, ending, as does the version from Matthew's Gospel, simply with 'And lead us not into temptation, but deliver us from evil' (Matt. 6:13). Even more disturbing to many people are the various modern translations which have rendered this prayer into the vernacular language: 'Our Father in heaven, hallowed be your name; your kingdom come, your will be done...' Sacrilege! Only Elizabethan English for this one, please! (The same with Psalm 23!)

---

[1] Contrary to what we might expect the *King James Version* uses 'debts' and 'debtors' (Matt. 6:12), going back to the Wycliffe translation of 1395, although later in the passage (Matt. 6:14–15) the *King James* does identify 'trespasses' as needing forgiveness. And the Anglican *Book of Common Prayer* (1662) uses 'trespasses.'

What a great pity, though. As it is with *Messiah* or the *Mona Lisa*, there are treasures upon treasures nestled in this prayer, if only we could get past the myths. There are good reasons why the *Lord's Prayer* has stood the test of time, but we hardly know the half of them. This modest volume seeks to repair the breach, in some small way. You may be thinking, has not everything already been said about this magnificent prayer? There are quite literally thousands of books about this prayer, and perhaps millions of sermons have been preached on it. Certainly, it would be foolish to ignore that heritage, for there is much to glean from it. Indeed, attempting complete originality would not only deprive us of some of the great insights of the past, but would be self-defeating, since the prayer is meant to be on the lips of believers in every generation, and thus to be understood afresh by God's people throughout history.

There are many ways to understand the *Lord's Prayer*, many of them quite legitimate. One is to see it as a model for the Christian life. A good number of the confessions and catechisms from the sixteenth and seventeenth centuries incorporate the *Lord's Prayer* as the best way to explicate the Christian life. For example, the prayer occupies a prominent place in the *Heidelberg Catechism* (1563). This catechism has a most significant outline. Divided into 52 'Lord's Days,' which can be, and often are, preached on in the evening services within a given year. After the magnificent opening statement on our 'only comfort in life and in death,' come three major sections: (1) Of Man's Misery; (2) Of Man's Redemption; and (3) Thankfulness. Significantly, this third section, about the Christian life, is a response to the gospel as outlined in the first two sections. In it our sanctification is considered an act of gratitude. Within that section, there is a teaching on dying to self, applying the ten commandments, and then, prayer, specifically, the *Lord's Prayer*, which is explained in Lord's Day 46-52, a total of ten Questions and Answers. The prayer is divided into an opening statement, followed by six petitions, and then a concluding statement. Thus the prayer serves to teach various elements of the Christian faith.

Similarly, the *Westminster Larger Catechism* uses the *Lord's Prayer* in a crucial way. The context is the defense of prayer as one of the chief means of grace (along with reading and preaching from the Word of God and the observance of the sacraments - Q & A 154). These practices are called the 'outward and ordinary means whereby Christ communicates to his church the benefits of his mediation.' Prayer is identified as 'an offering up of our desires unto God, in the name of Christ by the help of his Spirit' (Q & A 178). After several entries on the nature of prayer, the *Catechism* then asks, 'What rule hath God given for our direction in the duty of prayer?' (Q 186). The answer is, that 'The whole word of God is of use to direct us in the duty of prayer; but the special rule of direction is that form of prayer which our Saviour Christ taught his disciples, commonly called *The Lord's Prayer* (A 186). The *Catechism* further explains that not only is this prayer a pattern, but that it is appropriate, when done with understanding, to say the prayer itself. Like the *Heidelberg Catechism*, the *Westminster Larger Catechism* divides the prayer into a preface, followed by six petitions, then a conclusion. Each of these are carefully explained, always in relation to the Christian life.

In this little book, my purpose is not in any way to conflict with this traditional approach, which comes with a stamp of approval from the great traditions of the Reformation and the post-Reformation period of Protestant orthodoxy. However, I want to try and widen the outlook and consider the *Lord's Prayer* as more than a guide to our growth in piety, important as that may be. This extraordinary prayer is also an apologetic for the biblical worldview. Yet, in an age where confronting the world with such an all-encompassing approach might seem quaint at best, or irreverent at worst, I believe instead that this unique prayer offers us a remarkable statement of faith, as it stands opposed to a confused world. Cyprian called the prayer 'a compendium of heavenly doctrine.' Tertullian once called the *Lord's Prayer* 'an abridgement of the entire Gospel.'[2] Quite so! Of course, I do not want to sidestep the practical aspect of the prayer. If we achieved some sort of academic understanding of this prayer, but minimized the piety it is meant to inspire, then what a loss that would be. Rather, I am hoping for us to be able to hear it, and say it, afresh. As Marcel Proust once remarked, 'The real voyage of discovery consists not in seeking new landscapes, but in having new eyes.'

Prayer

Catechist: What desirest thou of God in this Prayer?

I desire my Lord God our heavenly Father, who is the giver of all goodness, to send His grace unto me, and to all people; that we may worship Him, serve Him, and obey Him, as we ought to do. And I pray unto God, that He will send us all things that be needful both for our souls and bodies; and that He will be merciful unto us, and forgive us our sins; and that it will please Him to save and defend us in all dangers ghostly and bodily; and that He will keep us from all sin and wickedness, and from our ghostly enemy, and from everlasting death. And this I trust He will do of His mercy and goodness, through our Lord Jesus Christ. And therefore I say, Amen, So be it.

(*Anglican Book of Common Prayer*, 1552)

---

[2] *Fathers of the Church*, vol. 40, 159; vol. 36, 133.

1

Why Pray at All?

> Prayer is an engine wieldable by every believer, mightier
> than all the embattled artillery of hell. Never out of season,
> nor to be deemed a drudgery, it is to be plied indefatigable,
> with a compass coextensive with the church universal.
>
> (E. K. Simpson & F. F. Bruce)

Guilt

Prayer is not often thought of as carrying a major philosophy
of life. Most people consider prayer to be connected with
worship, and making requests to God. And so it is. Or, they
consider prayer is what you do early in the morning, before
meals and just before going to bed. And so it should be. Prayer
in this sense is a habit, a good one. But few of us live the entire
reality of prayer. Few of us are in such regular conversation
with God. For many of us prayer is like the bread on each side
of a sandwich. It is like getting dressed each day. Prayer is like
punctuation. For the Lord Jesus and the heroes found in the
Bible, as we shall see, prayer is far, far more.

To be honest, the first reaction many of us have to the subject of prayer is guilt. Robert Murray McCheyne once said, 'You wish to humble a man? Ask him about his prayer life.' Very few of us pray as we should, whether in quantity or in quality. Yes, we make new resolutions from time to time to pray more, especially after something has prompted us: a crisis, a feeling of emptiness, a good book or sermon on prayer, observing a praying person, either from the past or in our present experience. But then the good intentions fade away and we are back into the busyness of living. Guilt! We have heard that Martin Luther prayed a good deal first thing in the morning, but when a really busy day was ahead of him, he got up even earlier to pray even more. Guilt! We may have read biographies of George Whitefield, in which we learn how he read God's Word on his knees and prayed over portions of it for hours on end. Guilt! Perhaps we are familiar with St. Teresa of Avila's nine grades of prayer: vocal, meditation, affective, simple, etc. Guilt! Or we may have paused over some of the extensive prayers recorded in Scripture. Think of Solomon's prayer at the dedication of the temple requiring 50 verses in 1 Kings 8, which we suspect was just a brief summary. Or, those wide-ranging Psalms which qualify as prayers. And, even though he railed against the long prayers of the Pharisees, Jesus himself prayed extensively. 'And rising very early in the morning, while it was yet dark, he departed and went to a desolate place, and there he prayed' (Mark 1:35). Guilt!

Guilt is not particularly productive nor constructive. It may provide an initial prodding, but then we need to move on to something not only positive but lasting. How can we find such a way? The answer is really quite simple. Not easy, but simple. If our prayer life is less than it should be, then likely it has little to do with discipline or method. Those are helpful, but they are beside the main problem. What is the main problem? Simply, our view of God is less than it should be. The greater our God, the more significant will be our prayer life. Put differently, it's all about our worldview, our vision. 'Prayer presupposes faith,' as the great French sociologist Jacques Ellul explains in his book on prayer. 'To raise the problem of prayer, of the difficulty of praying, etc., is in reality to raise the problem of faith in the contemporary world... Prayer is a mirror in which we are called to contemplate our spiritual state.'[1]

Two trends, particularly in the West, militate against a productive prayer life. The first is secularization. That word is loaded, and here is not the place to explore the concept as it deserves. Simply put, secularization means the functional absence of God in our lives. One legacy of the Enlightenment, though not the only one, is to believe we only need our unaided reason to function in life. If there is a God, he is in the gaps. Secularization means to think and live as though he were not really a significant factor, either intellectually or in practice.[2]

Before he became such a powerful voice into the twentieth century, Francis Schaeffer made a crucial discovery. He asked his wife, Edith, a haunting question: 'What if we woke up one morning and found our Bibles changed? What if God himself had removed everything in it about the Holy Spirit and prayer? What real difference would it make in our lives?' Precious little, they decided. The Schaeffers then resolved to live and act in the reality of God's presence. Indeed, the concept of *reality* is found everywhere in the Schaeffers' discourses and writings. Francis Schaeffer often referred to what he called the 'two chairs.' Christians can sit either in the 'chair of unfaith' or the 'chair of faith.' Being in the first chair does not mean you are an unbeliever, but that you do not operate in the light of the reality of the supernatural. In the chair of faith, you recognize the full reality of the supernatural world. You could be like the

---

[1] Jacques Ellul, *Prayer and Modern Man*, New York: Seabury Press, 1970, Introduction. [http://www.christinyou.net/pages/jacquesellul.html].

[2] The full story of secularization is rather more complicated. See Steve Bruce, *Secularization*, New York: Oxford University Press, 2011.

apostle Paul who had visited the 'third heaven' (2 Cor. 12:1-5). There he heard things that cannot be told (v. 4). Schaeffer asks us to imagine coming back down and seeing the world with new eyes. Living, then, in the chair of faith, prayer life will be greatly enhanced.[3]

The second trend is simply busyness. Although we only have ourselves to blame, the world demands more and more of our time for things that are means, not ends. How many of us are bound to various electronic leashes? Ask yourself, what did you do with your time prior to emails and texting? As most people do, I own a mobile phone. I even have an iPad. These devices are of course marvelously useful. But whereas I might have read a book, or talked to a real person, I now tend to send messages. I communicate rather than commune. I text rather than talk. And I notice myself being less and less patient with ordinary tasks, such as driving to the market, waiting for a letter, even walking through a museum. As Blaise Pascal told his seventeenth century readers, 'When all is equally agitated, nothing appears to be agitated, as in a ship. When all tend to debauchery, none appears to do so. He who stops draws attention to the excess of others, like a fixed point.'[4]

In such an atmosphere prayer is necessarily diminished. You simply cannot (and should not) *text* the Lord God. Prayer takes thought, and it takes time. Praying slowly and carefully can only be cultivated when we make time for doing it. Finding the time is more than a matter of getting up earlier, or making lists and carefully going through them. That may have to happen. But something more radical is needed. We will have to change our lifestyle so that such times for meditation are not just fit-

---

[3] See, for example, Francis A. Schaeffer, *Death in the City*, Wheaton: Crossway, 2002, 139-158. It is important to stress, as we will in a later chapter, that Schaeffer is not encouraging an unbiblical fascination with the supernatural, but is inviting us to take invisible forces, most of all God himself, seriously.

[4] *Pensées*, 382.

in, but are natural. Consider the ten commandments as guides for the Christian life. None of these commandments, rightly understood, are push-button. They can be accomplished externally, but that is not the point. Not committing murder, adultery or theft is far more than refraining from pulling the trigger, going to bed with the wrong person or embezzling funds. No, these 'rules' are guidelines for an entire way of life. They speak to our hearts. We need to be retrained in order to develop love and respect for our friends to the point where we are doing far more than avoiding maligning, cheating or ripping them off. Instead, we are enjoined to cultivate such a deep respect, such esteem and reverence for our neighbors, that we could not imagine taking advantage of them. Well, the same can be said for prayer. We don't just pray out of duty, resigning ourselves to God's command to pray. Instead, we should cultivate a love for conversing with the living God, the Lord who is ready to hear, and we should long for those times when we can speak our deepest thoughts to him. We ought to relish time for prayer, publically and privately, and feel frustrated when they are not abundant. Prayer, like matters of moral comportment, is a lifestyle issue.

And it takes an entire life to learn them. Apparently, after an astonishing concert, a fawning fan approached the great pianist Ignacy Paderewski, and told him, 'I would give my whole life to play the piano like you.' To which he answered, 'And that, dear friend, is exactly what it would take.' Most of us could not approach Paderewski's music after several lifetimes. But the point is, developing a habit, such as prayer, is a matter of a life commitment.

The first principle of prayer

Let us break down the components of prayer. First of all, it is we who pray. This may seem obvious. There is no coin to insert, no mouse to click, and no requisite spiritual posture to guarantee good praying. God does not pray in our stead. *We* pray. So, then what is prayer, considering the one who prays? Put one way, prayer is intercession. Human beings may intercede for one another. Lawyers intercede before the judge. Parents plead on behalf of their children. Similarly, praying to the Lord is to make intercession (1 Sam. 2:5; Isa. 59:16; Jer. 27:18). We even coin the term, 'intercessory prayer.' The word generally means to plead, or to liaise.

At the same time, prayer is not just any intercession. Prayer is the elevation of the soul to God. As Jean-Rodolphe Ostervald, pastor of the French church in Basel in the late seventeenth century, tells us about the nature of prayer in his marvelous book of daily devotions, 'King David says it best in Psalm 25:1, "To you, O Lord, I lift up my soul".' Ostervald reckons we learn about three aspects of prayer from these simple words. (1) Prayer must originate in our soul or in the heart, not merely on our lips. (2) Prayer must be addressed to the Lord, the true God, the only one able to hear us. (3) David's expression underscores the zeal, the ardor, the sincerity with which we must pray.[5]

Everything hinges on our attitude in praying. In a word, we want to pray in faith. Behind a healthy faith stands a healthy view of the world. Here is where our counter-cultural apologetics comes into play. An amusing story in the Book of Acts (12:1–19) illustrates how prayer can become perfunctory or routine. The apostle Peter had been locked up in a tight security prison for having preached the gospel. The church was earnestly praying for him. The night before his trial an angel came to the prison, woke Peter up, and guided him to the exit, as his chains miraculously fell off. The liberated Peter went to Mary's house and knocked on the door. There a prayer meeting was going on... for him! Rhoda, the house servant, went to answer, and recognized Peter's voice. In her joy she went back inside and proclaimed to the gathered group that he was free. They didn't believe her. 'You are out of your mind,' they told

[5] Jean-Rodolphe Ostervald, *La nourriture de l'âme*, Montbéliard : H. Barbier, 1766, 7.

her. It can't be true. He kept knocking. Finally they opened the door, and sure enough, it was Peter. What was happening here? They were saying, in effect, 'you can't be Peter, we've been praying for your release, but we know it is not likely to happen.'

The story is amusing but also convicting. How often do we pray for things, resigned that nothing much will happen? We assume nothing is going to change. Instead of believing in the living God for whom nothing is impossible, we have become functional fatalists. Perhaps, we believe, some force may govern events without much real care for our needs. The end of a war? Unrealistic. A hostile relative? He will never change. One of our French friends once told us that France would never respond to the gospel today. Astonished, we asked him how he knew that. His answer was, they have had their chance. When? At the Reformation. They started to respond but then turned their backs on the gospel, so God gave up on them.[6] Our friend had resigned himself to a world of no real change. He had forgotten that God does not rule as a grudging head of state, weary of his people. He does not give us just one chance, and then wash his hands. As long as the end of the world has not yet come, all people everywhere may still repent (Acts 17:30).

The same sentiment is behind the (musically beautiful) hymn, by James Lowell, 'Once to Every Man and Nation.' He wrote it in 1845, to protest America's war with Mexico.

> Once to every man and nation,
>   comes the moment to decide,
> In the strife of truth with falsehood,
>   for the good or evil side;
> Some great cause, some great decision,
>   offering each the bloom or blight,
> And the choice goes by forever,
>   'twixt that darkness and that light.

[6] The historical point, whether or how much French Protestants brought on the persecution themselves, is highly disputed.

Not very good poetry, the hymn goes on to plead for us to pursue the truth, no matter how costly. In all, these words are quite man-centered. Why only once? Why does the power to offer bloom or blight reside in humanity? The hymn is close to fatalism: once we make the wrong choice, we're locked-in.

In contrast, the biblical view informs us that we have a merciful God, always ready to hear us and shed his grace upon us.

> The Lord is merciful and gracious,
>> Slow to anger and abounding in steadfast love.
> He will not always chide,
>> Nor will he keep his anger forever.
> He does not deal with us according to our sins,
>> Nor repay us according to our iniquities...
> As a father shows compassion to his children,
>> So the Lord shows compassion on those who fear him
>> (Ps. 103:8–10, 13).

This Psalm is truly God-centered, though without minimizing human responsibility. Indeed, it is when we have a proper fear of God, and a confidence in his love, prayer begins to take on far more reality than any fatalism can explain. We need to make it clear that our prayers are effective not because of anything in the formulation, or even in the thoughts of our hearts, but because we have a merciful God, who gives us a first chance, a second chance, a third, fourth and on to the next time we cry out to him.

We might note with some interest how Paul appeals to us to pray in Ephesians 6. He uses the wonderful image of the soldier taking up the whole armor of God against rulers and spiritual forces, which has inspired many a preacher and many a story-teller: the belt of truth, the breastplate of righteousness, the shoes of the gospel, the shield of faith, the helmet of salvation, and the sword of the Spirit are the indispensable protective covering for the believer doing battle with the enemies of the kingdom (Eph. 6:13–17). But it is significant, is it not, that prayer is not among the portions of the armor? One of the reasons is surely that prayer is so important, it is not on the list, but treated separately. More than these accoutrements, prayer is simply fundamental: 'praying at all times in the Spirit, with all prayer and supplication for all the saints, and also for me...' (Eph. 6:18).

Thus, prayer is intercession. It is we who pray, not God praying for us. Yet our earthly intercession only makes sense if the God to whom we pray is ready to listen, full of mercy and grace.

Three powerful intercessors

So, prayer is lifting up the soul. We pray. It is our intercession. Yet, according to the Christian worldview, we are not alone as intercessors. Indeed, what allows our prayers to be effective is not primarily our human agency, important though that may be. Rather it is the intercession of God, the Holy Trinity. Though one in essence, our God exists in three separate Persons. Their purpose, while united, is also expressed through each of the Persons in a particular way. God the Father cares about the needs of his people. God the Son opens up the way into his heavenly presence. And God the Holy Spirit applies all of the Lord's grace to every area of our lives, particularly to efficacy in prayer.

(1) God the Father. Thus we can understand something of the relation of our human, earthly intercession, with God's heavenly intercession. God the Father is the holy judge of the universe. But he is also infinitely gracious and merciful. What matters to us also matters to God. So we come confidently to him. We come as advocates, interceding on behalf of people or concerns. At the same time, our concerns become the Father's concerns. To illustrate the need to intercede with perseverance in the face of a God who cares about us, Jesus told the story of the importunate widow (Luke 18:1–8). Though the judge in this story was hard-hearted, the woman kept coming to him,

insisting that he hear her case. Finally he responded, weary of her pleas. God, Jesus taught, is far more responsive than a sedentary judge. He is a Father. He cares for his people. He will come just when it is right, without undue delay, because he hears their cry, day and night. If human magistrates need to be prodded to rescue widows, God is particularly sensitive to the plight of widows, orphans and aliens, as he tells us repeatedly in his Word. When our prayers are perfunctory, that would be for one of two reasons. Perhaps we have ceased caring for our cause. Or, worse, it could be because we have ceased believing God really wants to respond.

We often have a vision of God as a fitful tyrant. Certainly he is a judge and it is proper to fear him with reverence. But the Bible describes him as a Father, one who is generous with his children. The preacher and theologian Sinclair Ferguson likes to say God saves, not reluctantly, but relentlessly. Indeed, Jesus told his disciples that if even earthly fathers who are sinners know how to give good gifts to his children, how much more will the heavenly Father give us the very best. Luke records it this way: 'If you then, who are evil, know how to give good gifts to your children, how much more will the heavenly Father give the Holy Spirit to those who ask him! (Luke 11:13). God rewards those who seek him (Heb. 11:6); he is just that kind of God. So God himself is our intercessor. But there is more to it than simply that.

(2) God the Son. Gloriously, God the Son has become our major access to God. The Son became a man, and opened the way for our entrance into God's presence. The entire Old Testament tells of the way God came down to earth in order to bring his people into his presence. Various images help explain this journey. The people were to build a temple for the Lord to dwell in, a place where he could meet with them. Going up to Jerusalem on special occasions was a joyful parade, leading to Mount Zion and then to the temple. The people sang the Songs of Ascent (Psalms 120–134) as they marched.

The problem when they arrived is that no one could enter the most holy place inside. The high priest could, but only once a year, having performed a blood sacrifice for himself and for the people. The final fulfillment of this picture is Jesus Christ, who entered Jerusalem in triumph, on a colt, with the crowds singing from Psalm 118. Then he was put to death, rising from the dead on the first Easter Sunday.

Now Jesus is our true high priest. As the Book of Hebrews argues forcefully, Jesus not only went into the holy of holies, but gave us access to the throne of grace (Heb. 4:14; 9:11-14). Because he suffered so, he understands us. He sympathizes. He makes propitiation for us (Heb. 2:17-18). Because of his once and for all death on Calvary's cross, this propitiation applies in the present. He is our advocate with the Father and the propitiation for our sins (1 John 2:1-2). The Father always hears him, not only because he is his eternal Son, but because he perfectly obeyed him in his life and death on earth (Heb. 5:8-10). He did this all for us, his beloved people. In what we call the 'High Priestly Prayer,' recorded in John 17, Jesus prays to the Father and makes all of these connections. He asked for his people, reminding the Father that he perfectly accomplished all that was required of him. Now that he is about to depart the world, through death, he entrusts his people to the Father's care. And the Father is delighted to answer him. Indeed, the whole purpose of the Son's incarnation, of his death and resurrection, was to give us access to God's grace (Rom. 5:2). And this open door makes the success of our prayers assured. And there is still more to it than even this wonderful truth.

(3) God the Holy Spirit. As if this provision were not enough, the third Person of the Trinity is also here to intercede for us. If the Father is the one who welcomes us, and if Christ is our heavenly advocate, we also have an earthly one, the Spirit of God. John extensively records the last teachings of Christ to his disciples in what we know as the Upper Room Discourse (John 13-17). Here Jesus promised the disciples that when

he went away he and the Father would make their home with believers (John 14:23). He does that by the Holy Spirit whom he sends in his name. The Spirit is called our Helper (in the King James, the Comforter, see John 14:16, 26; 15:26; 16:7). The Greek word is *paraclete* which can mean helper or comforter, but also has a more juridical connotation. The Spirit is an advocate, a counselor, an intercessor. The Holy Spirit is the agent of God's presence and strength in the life of the church. He seals us in Christ, so that our inheritance is sure (Eph. 1:13-14). He gives us new life, resurrection life, and sets us free to please God, which we cannot do by nature (Rom. 8:2, 9-11, 15).

And, most important for our purposes, he helps us to pray:

> Likewise the Spirit helps us in our weakness. For we do not know how to pray as we ought, but the Spirit himself intercedes for us with groaning too deep for words. And he who searches hearts knows what is the mind of the Spirit because the Spirit intercedes for the saints according to the will of God (Rom. 8:26-27).

The context for this statement is the sufferings of the present life. God gives us hope, to encourage us through our sufferings (vv. 18-25). And he gives the Holy Spirit to encourage us through our longing for the new heaven and the new earth. Paul addresses us in our weakness. We are no doubt weak in every matter pertaining to perseverance, but here he stresses our inability to pray as we should. To highlight prayer is to underscore the very heart of what it is to be a Christian. To pray is to commune with God. Other aspects of the Christian life matter, certainly, but prayer is our direct line to the Father. Prayer is also the hardest activity to practice, because talking to God is where we are most weak. The remedy? Not tips on what to say, nor on our posture, nor on the hour we should pray. Rather, the remedy is the activity of the Holy Spirit. John Murray reminds us, 'Too seldom has the intercessory activity of the Holy Spirit been taken into account. The glory of

Christ's intercession should not be allowed to place the Spirit's intercession in eclipse.'[7]

What does the Holy Spirit do with our prayers? There is some mystery here. His groaning may be too deep for words but that is not to say that they are devoid of content. Nor should it be thought they are unconnected with our own human inward groaning (v. 23). These expressions certainly do not refer to special gifts such as speaking in tongues. What they are saying is that the Holy Spirit in his great power and wisdom is able to transform our inadequate prayers into prayers that the Father will hear and approve. Just as God knows the hearts of his creatures, so he knows the mind of the Holy Spirit who, in this case, takes our prayers and shapes them so that they accord with his own will. That is why, in another portion of Scripture, we are told, 'if we ask anything according to his will he hears us,' and answers (1 John 5:14-15). So, then, we intercede, but in the end, God intercedes for us.

Why pray?

God is utterly sovereign. So why pray? Are human beings in any way significant? Do their prayers matter? The answer is yes, a thousand times, yes. Prayer is indeed one of the most important proofs of the double truth, God ordains everything, our actions make a difference. Prayer depends on both the sovereignty of God and the significance of human beings. While the ultimate connection between the two is mysterious (to us!), still, both must be affirmed. Indeed, human significance is *required* by the kind of sovereign God is. Without being determinists nor fatalists, we affirm that God is fully in control of everything, including his commitment to human dignity. Both sides are often stated together in Scripture, without raising a theological or logical issue. For example, Jesus forbids empty phrases in

[7] John Murray, *The Epistle to the Romans*, vol. 1, Grand Rapids: Eerdmans, 1959, 311–312.

prayer, adding the 'your Father knows what you need before you ask him' (Matt. 6:7–8). Well then, you might ask, why pray? No such question is raised here. The only answer given is to pray sincerely, even secretly before the 'audience of One.' God hears and responds to our prayers when they are said authentically. The fact that he knows what we will say before we say it does not subtract at all from our need to pray. In another example, Matthew records Jesus saying (actually praying with gratitude) that God hides things from the 'wise and understanding' while revealing them to little children (Matt. 11:25). He then turns around and invites *anyone* who has a burden to come to him for rest (v. 28). If you followed either thought to its logical conclusion you would end up with a dilemma. In John chapter 6, twice Jesus makes reference to God drawing his people to himself (vv. 37, 44). And twice he refers to the role of human will, or faith (vv. 47, 53–54).

One of the most striking illustrations of our double truth is by Paul, describing the Christian life to the Philippians:

> Therefore, my beloved, as you have always obeyed, so now, not only as in my presence but much more in my absence, work out your own salvation in fear and trembling, for it is God who works in you, both to will and to work for his good pleasure (Phil. 2:12–13).

A lot is going on here. Paul is away. He is in jail, actually. So he is anxious for his converted friends to keep growing, on their own. The word translated 'work out' is the same one from which we get our technical term for measuring energy: *ergs*. Expend your strength, he is saying, in a strong statement of human responsibility. At the same time, all due credit is given to God. 'For it is God who works in you,' he states, without embarrassment. This time the word for 'work' is the Greek term for *energy* itself. God is energizing you both to will and to work for his good pleasure, he tells us. To our modern question, 'so, which is it, us or God?' Paul would simply answer, 'yes!' Although he does not spell out the link here, he does say our work is done in fear and trembling. That is a biblical expression. It can mean being terrorized. But it also often refers to an attitude of humility, or simply of faith (Ps. 2:11; 2 Cor. 7:15; Eph. 6:5). Even our working should not presume that it is all because of our good merits. Further, a better translation of verse 12 might say, 'work out of your own salvation.' We are saved by grace; now live out the implications of that. God's work gives us incentive to work. Our work is an index of God's work.

The one place where this relationship does seem to raise a theological issue is in Romans 9, where Paul is discussing the deep reasons why many Jews did not respond to the gospel. After some strong statements on God's election ('I will have mercy upon whom I have mercy'), he anticipates the question: 'You will say to me, then, "Why does he still find fault? For who can resist his will?"' (v. 19). He then comes back with even stronger statements on God's sovereignty: 'Has the potter no right over the clay?' Even here, though, Paul is not describing a determinist God. While he is certainly lifting the veil and letting us glimpse at the ultimate control over human affairs, he nevertheless fully recognizes human responsibility. Paul is not saying, in effect, 'shut up and worship,' although he does admonish those who doubt God's fairness. Instead, he argues, not for human finitude, but for human guilt. Presupposed throughout the whole passage is human fallenness. Only in a sinful world does the grace of God to some, though not to everyone, make any sense. God could well have left every human being under judgment and been perfectly right to do so. Yet he has mercy on many. The term *mercy* is telling: underserved grace for those who should have been condemned. Even the language of the potter and the clay is significant. Clay is a biblical image for human beings in their weakness. The potter takes many sinners, fragile, earthen vessels, and moulds them into beautiful pots. But not all.

Why not? Here is the mystery. There is nothing unfair about not saving everyone, when God did not have to save anyone. Still, we may ask, as did Paul's readers, why did not everyone believe? The passage actually deals with the question, why did the Jews not all come to Christ? The question is deeply disturbing to Paul, a Jew himself, who could wish himself cut off if it could mean the Jews responding in greater numbers (9:1-4). And he defends the power of the Word of God, which cannot fail (v.6). We can fail, but not the Word. We just do not know why God chooses many but not all. We simply do not know. But this is the way it is. And because God is so wonderfully loving, whatever the reasons for his passing some by, they cannot be divorced from his character, which is profoundly good. The wonder is that he saves at all, and not only a few, but many!

All of this is to say that God is utterly powerful, and we are utterly responsible. Here is how the *Westminster Confession of Faith* puts it:

> God from all eternity, did, by the most wise and holy counsel of his own will, freely and unchangeably ordain whatsoever comes to pass: yet so, as thereby neither is God the author of sin, nor is violence offered to the will of the creatures; nor is the liberty or contingency of second causes taken away, but rather established (III.1).

God is powerful beyond words. Yet (notice the crucial hinge words, *yet so*) he is not the instigator of sin, nor does he violate the creatures he has made. Rather than interfering with their decision-making, he *establishes* a world in which secondary causes are significant.

The great principle here, then, is that we pray because an all-powerful God has made us significant (establishing our liberty). He has made us with the ability to relate to him, in praise or in humility or in our requests. The wonder of who we are testifies to his generosity as the Creator. He no doubt could have made us robots. Instead, he made us after his image, able to rule, able to speak and understand, able to decide between right and wrong. He wants us not only to worship him as he deserves, but to commune and converse with him. He has even called us his *friends* (John 15:15). When we pray, then, we are adoring our Creator, but we are also addressing our God in friendship. Abraham was called the friend of God, and so it is of us (James 2:23). This friendship is with a difference. No earthly person can require the kind of friendship which worships and serves them. Still, when we pray to God, among other things, we come as his friends. We now may have the same kind of communion with God that the Son has with the Father (John 17:11; 1 John 1:3). Amazing!

Prayer and faith

Does this mean that anything we ask will be granted? On the surface, it would seem so. Jesus told his disciples, 'whatever you ask in prayer, you will receive, if you have faith' (Matt. 21:22; Mark 11:24). Again, in the Upper Room Discourse, Jesus assures his disciples, 'whatever you ask in my name, this I will do' (John 14:3; 15:7, 16; 16:23). But this does not seem to square with our experience. What about unanswered prayer? Some pious people will tell you God always answers your prayer, just not always in the way you had hoped. Perhaps so. But then how helpful is it to be told such a thing, if you are really trying to pray sincerely and nothing seems to happen? Some will tell you, just always add the qualifier, 'if it be your will.' That seems safe enough, and it's a biblical teaching as well (1 John 5:14). Maybe it is too safe. 'Lord, please bring peace so that your people may cease from being persecuted, *if that be your will.*' This sounds like a request to a fatalist god, not to the God of the Bible who listens caringly to his people and who cares deeply about the persecution of his people. Besides, he has expressly told us it *is* his will that there be peace, and that he will bring it about (Col. 1:20; Phil. 4:7).

However, we don't need to jettison this phrase altogether. 'If it be your will' is actually much more involved than figuring out whether or not God agrees with my request. Stephen Smalley helps us understand the deeper meaning of this concept. 'There is nothing mechanical or magical about prayer. For it to be effective, the will of the intercessor needs to be in line with the will of God; and such a conformity of wills is brought about only as the believer lives in Christ.'[8] Thus, prayer is not a push-button matter. It begins with the understanding that our whole way of life is involved. Smalley adds, 'The fundamental characteristic of all truly Christian intercession is that the will of the person who offers the prayer should coincide with God's will. Prayer is not a battle, but a response; its power consists of lifting our wills to God, not in trying to bring his will down to us.'[9]

So, what happens when peace does not come? Let us go deeper into the issue of requests and answers. First, it is clear, God being sovereign, that he reserves the right to answer as he pleases. And he may not answer our prayer as formulated. Or, perhaps, his answer might be in a very different direction from what we have prayed for. Why would this be? Several reasons suggest themselves. For one thing, some prayers are simply not legitimate, and God, mercifully, will not answer them. Jonah asked God to take his life away; but he did not (Jon. 4:3). Jonah had a mission to accomplish and even he, the missionary, could not abort it, though he tried. Two disciples requested to be able to sit next to Jesus in his glory. They not only received a very different answer ('[this] is not mine to grant') but a promise that they must suffer a great deal before entering into heaven (Mark 10:35-44). For another, some prayers are more legitimate, yet in his wisdom God does not answer them in the way they are expressed. We may think of David, who prayed fervently that the son he had with Bathsheba would

[8] Stephen S. Smalley, *1, 2, 3 John: Word Biblical Commentary*, vol. 51, Waco, TX: Word Books, 1984, 205.

[9] Ibid., 295.

live. But he did not (2 Sam. 12:13–23). Was his prayer wrong? Certainly not, but God chose not to agree with the prayer. We are not altogether sure why. Perhaps David needed to feel the full force of the consequences for his adultery. But we are not told this, and it is not wise to guess at it.

In some cases we do know why some particular prayers, even legitimate ones, are not answered as formulated. Paul prayed that the thorn in his flesh be removed. He prayed fervently, but in this case the Lord wanted him to rely entirely on the sufficiency of his grace (2 Cor. 12:7–10). There is nothing wrong with praying for relief or healing. We are encouraged to do so. James tells us in the strongest terms to pray for those who are suffering. 'And the prayer of faith will save the one who is sick, and the Lord will raise him up,' he adds (James 5:13–15). He reminds his readers of Elijah, a man of flesh and bones, just like us, whose prayer could make the rain come and go (vv. 17–18). But neither was Paul's prayer for relief from his thorn in the flesh answered, nor are a number of our legitimate prayers answered as we could have wished. In Paul's case there was a better way. He needed to learn afresh how God's grace is sufficient, and how his power is made perfect in weakness (2 Cor. 12:9). When this principle is communicated with great sensitivity, it is comforting for those of us who may be suffering, and plead with God for relief. Relief is good. Full knowledge of God's grace is better.

Prayer, together with the possible absence of the kind of answer we wish for, leads us far deeper into God's purposes than if we simply required him to show up and perform. Consider the case for lasting peace. While God promises to bring peace, he also tells us to ask for it, recognizing that peace is never automatic. In almost every opening greeting, Paul (and the other apostles) wish for peace, the peace of God, upon the congregations (Gal. 1:3; Eph. 1:2; Phil. 1:2; Col. 1:2; 1 Pet. 1:2). Throughout the New Testament, peace is enjoined as a goal to strive for, not a *fait accompli* (Col. 3:15;

1 Thess. 5:13; 2 Thess. 3:16; 2 Tim. 2:22; Heb. 12;14, etc.). There are even warnings against a false sense of peace and security (Jer. 6:14; Ez. 13:10; Luke 21:34; 1 Thess. 5:3). So, we can see there is a complex set of realities, no one of which controls the others in any push-button sense. Yes, we should pray for peace. And yes, God will bring it. But he will do so on his own terms, making sure that first things are first.

There are still other reasons why the Lord may not answer our prayers precisely in the terms of our requests. A crucial reason is timing. Why is timing so crucial? Many reasons suggest themselves. Sometimes to answer a prayer immediately could spoil everything. The intricacy of God's Providence means he is working all things for good. Yet this means a worldview in which everything, that is, everything, concerts together for God's good purposes. This requires just the right sets of circumstances so that the good is produced, not only for the one praying, but for the Christian community and even the entire world. Vaclav Havel, who, after a long period of detention by the communists, was released and became president of Czechoslovakia (then of the Czech Republic), was criticized for not moving fast enough to undo the damage of communism and establish a complete democracy. He chided his critics, saying that if you rush things you may become like the child, trying desperately to make his flower grow by pulling it from the stem, only to find it breaks. Timing is everything!

The way God answers prayer, whether positively or negatively, always involves the deeper issue of how we relate to him. When Jacob fought with the angel all night, he received a wounded hip from it. Then he was renamed Israel ('Wrestler with God'). What an image! He had seen God face to face and lived, yet it cost him his health (Gen. 32:22–32). Likewise, when we pray we are wrestling with the living God, not clicking a mouse or paying a vending machine. So, when we pray, all kinds of things are happening. We pray expectantly, as we must. But God responds in ways far more beneficial, far more gracious than we could imagine. He 'wrestles us down,' so that we become far more dependent, and far more sanctified than we might have were we in full control.

The Orthodox priest Anthony Bloom makes the sobering reflection that when prayer goes unanswered, it appears God himself is absent. Any kind of mechanical remedy that tries to force God on us is doomed to failure, because both God and we are alive: 'The fact that God can make Himself present or can leave us with a sense of His absence is part of this live and real relationship. If we could mechanically draw Him into an encounter, force Him to meet us, simply because we have chosen this moment to meet Him, there would be no relationship and no encounter.'[10] He goes on to describe some of the possible reasons for the seeming absence of God: guilt feelings, our own coldness, indifference toward God, except when we think we really need him, etc.

God rules the world as omnipotent, but also as a divine Person, who is anxious to have our friendship! Our faith, then, grows, when he wrestles with us. Faith is not a once-for-all gift. It begins decisively, but then it continues to grow and grow. Faith is ours, but it ultimately comes by the grace of God (Eph. 2:8). Faith must deepen. Such deepening often occurs through trials. James makes the connection: 'Count it all joy, my brothers, when you meet trials of various kinds. For you know that the testing of your faith produces steadfastness' (James 1:2). Peter puts it this way: 'In this [power of grace] you rejoice, though now for a little while, as was necessary, you have been grieved by various trials, so that the genuineness of your faith—more precious than gold that perishes though it is tested by fire—may be found to result in praise and glory and honor at the revelation of Jesus Christ' (1 Pet. 1:6–7).

Do we know God so well that we can feel him wrestling against us? Or is he merely a concept, a series of doctrines

---

[10] Anthony Bloom, *Beginning to Pray*, New York, Mahwah: Paulist Press, 1970, 26.

about attributes, Persons and essence? Depending on the answer, prayer is everything to us, or it is nothing!

Prayer

Gracious and holy Father,
please give me:
Intellect to understand you;
Reason to discern you;
Diligence to seek you;
Wisdom to find you;
A spirit to know you;
A heart to meditate upon you;
Ears to hear you;
Eyes to see you;
A tongue to proclaim you;
A way of life pleasing to you;
Patience to wait for you; and
Perseverance to look for you.

(A prayer of Benedict, 480–547 AD)

2

The Setting for the Lord's Prayer

It was not unusual for rabbis to teach specific prayers. Notice that the text treats prayer as a learned experience, not simply as a release of feelings. Discipline is clearly implied. (Fred B. Craddock)

The *Lord's Prayer* is rendered in two places in the New Testament: Matthew 6:9–13 and Luke 11:2–4. Of course, although we call it the *Lord's* prayer, our Lord Jesus could never have prayed it, for at least two reasons. First, it addresses God as *Our* Father. While Jesus taught the Fatherhood of God, he always distinguished between his own Father, from whom he was begotten, and God the Father of believers. When he appeared to Mary Magdalene after his resurrection, Jesus told her that he would be ascending 'to my Father and your Father, to my God and your God' (John 20:17). Although Christ is not ashamed to call us brothers (Heb. 2:11–12) that does not mean that God is our Father in quite the same way as he is for him. The second reason is that the prayer asks God to forgive our debts, that is, our sins (Matt. 6:12; Luke 11:4). Jesus was in every way like us, except he was without sin (Heb. 4:15). In view of these thoughts it might better be called the *Disciples' Prayer*. But we can stay with the traditional name, particularly because it was given to us by Jesus Christ himself, who is the Lord.

The *Lord's Prayer*, then, is Christ's gift to his people. And what a superb gift it is! According to one of the earliest testimonies to liturgical life in the church, the *Didache*, the *Lord's Prayer* and the Lord's Supper are two great treasures given by the Lord to believers. To pray the *Prayer* is a great privilege.[1]

Here are the two from the ESV translation:

Matthew 6:9–13	Luke 11:2–4
Our Father in heaven, hallowed be your name.	Father, hallowed be your name.
Your kingdom come, your will be done, on earth as it is in heaven.	Your kingdom come.
Give us this day our daily bread,	Give us each day our daily bread,
and forgive us our debts, as we also have forgiven our debtors.	And forgive us our sins, For we ourselves forgive everyone who is indebted to us.
And lead us not into temptation, but deliver us from evil.	And lead us not into temptation.

Why the two versions? While we are not sure altogether, it is likely that Jesus reiterated the basic form of the prayer several times, as the occasion warranted it. The version given in Matthew is fuller, and the phrases suggest it had begun to belong to the liturgy of the church. In Luke the prayer is much shorter, and is in direct response to the question posed by the

---

[1] See, Joachim Jeremias, *The Lord's Prayer*, Philadelphia: Fortress Press, 1964, 5.

disciples, after watching Jesus pray: 'Lord, teach us to pray' (11:1). Matthew addresses a primarily Jewish audience, which means he is interacting with the Jewish mindset, whereas Luke is addressing more of a mixed audience, including the Gentiles. So, for example, Matthew may have focused on Jewish sensitivities to the way God's name is used. Thus, the first petition says, 'Our Father who is in heaven, hallowed be your name,' circumscribing God's divinity, whereas Luke's version says simply, 'Father, hallowed be your name.' (Similarly, in Matthew, the kingdom of God is referred to as the kingdom of heaven, so the reference to 'as it is in heaven'.) Again, Matthew asks that we be forgiven our debts, 'as we also have forgiven our debtors,' using a Greek mood (the aorist) which means something like, 'as we also now herewith forgive our debtors.' Luke, instead uses the present, 'as we forgive our debtors.'[2] We should not make too much of these differences, since, after all, we are discussing the same basic prayer.

Matthew

The context in the first Gospel is the Sermon on the Mount, where Jesus gives a compendium of teaching to the assembled crowd along with the disciples. While the Sermon resembles the wise teachings of the Sage in Israel, it is a commentary on God's law from a New Covenant perspective. Fundamentally, the Sermon explains what life in Christ is to be like. Jesus has not come to abolish the Law and the Prophets, that is, the body of teaching found in the Old Testament. Instead, he has come to fulfill that body (Matt. 5:17). The Greek word here is *pleiroo*. The idea is that Jesus has come to accomplish the law, not abrogate it. Two things are involved. First, keeping the law, sustaining it, endorsing it. Second, taking it to its deepest level.

John captures this double feature of the New Covenant well, when he says, 'Beloved, I am writing you no new commandment,

---

[2] Ibid., 14

but an old commandment...' Then he says, 'At the same time, it is a new commandment... which is true in him...' (1 John 2:7–8). From now on, the old has become renewed in Christ. John adds that now 'the darkness is passing away and the true light is already shining' (v. 8). We sense the tremendous freshness of the gospel. Faith is for anyone who has eyes to see, not just the elite. While everything in the Sermon on the Mount is hard, because it requires such authenticity, yet Jesus Christ gives the grace and power to practice the radical righteousness of the new era. And it is there for anyone who asks: 'For everyone who asks receives and the one who seeks finds, and to the one who knocks it will be opened.' The reason this can happen? The generosity of our good-hearted heavenly Father! (Matt. 7:7–11).

Only when you build your house on the rock of believing and practicing this teaching can you endure the judgment (7:24–27). In doing so Jesus shows how deep and how spiritual God's ways are, compared to the prevailing views of official Judaism. Jewish religion had largely become external, legalistic, and ritualistic. Much of the Sermon is counter-cultural in light of that local religion. Jesus' message is both a corrective against legalism and a step forward. A corrective, because it pushes back against the rote practices of the Jewish leadership, which led to an elitism that kept ordinary people from faith. A step forward because from now on, all religious behavior was to be practiced in Christ, by Christ's power and for Christ's sake.

Beginning with the *Beatitudes*, the Sermon assures believers that they are blessed, given God's outpouring of grace and love in the midst of hardship, poverty and persecution (Matt. 5:2–12). So we can see right from the beginning how this message is a corrective: the *Beatitudes* concentrate on our identity, on who we are, rather than what we do. But it is also a step forward, because no one had ever quite stated things this way. Not the rich or the well-established, but those who mourn, who desperately seek his righteousness, those who show mercy, they will know God's favor. The Sermon goes on to show the many ways that such personal integrity is a fundamentally different approach from the typical religion of the day. Culpable anger is much more than physically killing someone (5:21–26). Lust is far deeper than the act of adultery (5:27–30). Enemies should receive our love and not retaliation (5:38–48). The rest of the message explains some of the major implications of being blessed believers in Christ.

The *Lord's Prayer* is nestled in with a series of thoughts about cultivating a genuine life before God, rather than trying to impress people. 'Beware of practicing your righteousness before other people in order to be seen by them,' the section opens up. When you do that you will have no benefit from God. You will have a reward, but it is meagerly compared to the reward of friendship with God. Paid in full! But how empty.

Do we not have the same problem today? One of the insights in Lloyd Douglas' novel, *Magnificent Obsession*, is how to cultivate an authentic secret life. About half way through the tale, the young Dr. Wayne Hudson has lost his beloved wife. 'On the edge of failure and in deep depression,' he goes to the monument works to pick a marker for her grave. There he meets an eccentric but gifted sculptor, Clive Randolph. Perceiving the doctor's state of mind, Randolph begins a conversation with him, which leads to a friendship. He explains that he has a great secret which can transform his life. Here it is. Most of us live *depleted* lives, and we are zestless. We slouch toward pessimism, fear, and despondency. The reason is, according to the sculptor, that when we do a good deed, we want others to know, so we display it somewhere. This gives us some joy—immediate gratification. We get credit. But it doesn't last. On the other hand, when we do something cheap and mean-spirited, we hide it or deny it. So, ironically, we start a tab, we accumulate our 'credit.' But soon we find ourselves spiritually bankrupt, because this kind of reward doesn't mean much.

What if, instead, Randolph continues, we reversed our strategy? What if, whenever we did something good, we hid it? And whenever we did the wrong thing, we advertized it (appropriately)? This will give us wonderful power, he argues. Where did he get such a marvelous idea? He went to church with his daughter and heard (we imagine—we are not told) Matthew 6, and came away wanting to try the new principle out in his own life. From then on he concealed anything good he might have done, and confessed his misdeeds to those whom he had offended. Randolph had been, up until the church incident, a competent, but ordinary stone cutter. Suddenly, he became a famous sculptor, exhibiting his works in the best museums. Dr. Hudson also tried the experiment. He kept all his giving to charities secret. And he not only overcame his depression but became one of the most famous surgeons of his day.

The lesson to take away here is not so much that we might become famous if we were more modest. Rather, it is the profound biblical truth that what matters most is not what other people see in us, but who we are inwardly. Hobart Mowrer, the remarkable psychologist and originator of 'integrity therapy' (later, 'reality therapy') was inspired by Lloyd Douglas. After analysing *Magnificent Obsession*, he concluded, 'we *are* our secrets.'[3] Many have observed the same truth. Thomas Babington Macaulay once said, 'The measure of a man's real character is what he would do if he knew he would never be found out.' What matters most is who we are in secret, in a word, our motives. La Rochefoucauld once said, 'If the world were aware of the motives behind them, we would often be ashamed of our finest actions.'[4] The Sermon on the Mount shines a bright light on our souls. If the picture is not very pretty, the Sermon also tells us how to clean it up.

The immediate context for the *Lord's Prayer* within the Sermon is in a section devoted to prayer. Once more, Jesus

---

[3] Hobart Mowrer, *The New Group Therapy*, Albany: Van Nostrand Reinhold, 1964, 71.

[4] From 'When No One Sees,' The Trinity Forum, 2000, 4–34.

contrasts this *secret* approach to that of the group he calls 'the hypocrites.' While not naming them, it is likely that he refers to the Scribes and the Pharisees, constant objects of his indignation. Apparently many Jews would pause at about 3pm to offer prayers tied in with the evening sacrifice in the temple. Although the content of these prayers was not prescribed, many said them loud, and in a public place so that passersby could see them. He also aims at the Gentiles' methods (Matt. 6:7). Perhaps he was thinking of pagans in the Old Testament, such as the prophets of Baal who 'called upon the name of Baal from morning until night' (1 Kings 18:26). Or he may have been thinking of the Gentiles who hovered around the Jews in his own day, some of them 'seekers,' but others merely onlookers trying to benefit from their religious practices. Matthew, as well as other Gospel writers, often refers to the Gentiles. Sometimes it is negatively, as here. For example, Jesus teaches the disciples that the practice of authority by the Gentiles is by power and elitism, not service (Matt. 20:25). Later, as they entered Jerusalem, he told his disciples that he would be a victim of the Scribes and Pharisees and 'be delivered over to the Gentiles' (20:19). At other times, the Gentiles are put in a better light. They would be receiving the Gospel (10:18; 12:18, 21). Jesus several times alluded to the positive response of the Gentiles to his message, at times a better one than the Jews evidenced (15:22-28). Still, in all these cases the Gentiles are seen as outsiders, in keeping with the Old Testament mentality.

Jew and Gentile alike are condemned when they pray only to be seen and heard by others. We should not conclude from this that Jesus condemns all public prayer, or even prayer that uses some repetition. Jesus himself prayed publically (11:25). And he repeated his plea with the Father that he be spared the cross three times in the Garden of Gethsemane (26:44). The point here is that we should pray sincerely, and if it means hiding away so that no one but God hears you, then hide away. When it really dawns on us that God is present, that he knows our thoughts, and that he is not impressed by our rituals and formulas, then we are ready to pray from the heart. In the Old Testament the fool is contrasted with the wise person because he uses too many words (Prov. 10:19; Eccles. 5:3). So, the *Lord's Prayer*, among other things, is an efficient prayer. No babbling.

Luke

The rendering of the *Lord's Prayer* in Luke (11:2–4) is not divorced from concerns about authenticity. Jesus had just sent the disciples on a mission, to proclaim the Good News to several cities (10:1–24). Wherever they went they were to preach the Kingdom of God in its saving and healing power. Should the town reject the message, the consequences would be severe (Sodom would get a lighter sentence on the day of judgment). To reject the disciples is to reject Jesus, and to reject Jesus is to reject the God who sent him (v. 16). This mission was of the utmost importance. It came with power to destroy Satan. Nevertheless, the disciples were to rejoice in something better than such power: that their names were written in heaven (v. 20). At the end of the mission, Jesus gathers his disciples and says to them: 'Blessed are the eyes that see what you see!' Even prophets and kings had longed to see what they saw (vv. 23–24).

Francis Schaeffer, as we have mentioned, struggled to find spiritual reality in his life. How can our Christian lives be more genuine? Again, he takes us to the apostle Paul's experience of visiting the 'third heaven' (2 Cor. 12:1–6). Paul is reluctantly defending the genuineness of his apostolic authority against his Corinthian critics. Remember, he has been raptured into Paradise. Here is the very Schaefferian way he comments on Paul's experience:

> Can't you imagine this man as he came back from heaven? He had seen it as a propositional truth, as a brute fact. He had been there, and looked at it, and then had come back. Would anything ever have looked the same to him again? It

is as though he had died. It is as though he had been raised from the dead. Just as the Mount of Transfiguration gives us a different perspective when we are in the perspective of the Kingdom of God, how different this man's perspective would have been all his life... What would the praise of the world be worth when one had stood in the presence of God? The wealth of the world, what would it look like beside the treasures of heaven?[5]

In a profound way, praying the *Lord's Prayer* means our eyes have been opened to the reality of heaven, and of the entire supernatural world. If we have seen this then our gaze at the world can never be the same. Surely, it is no coincidence that Luke inserts the prayer into this portion of his text.

Following the missions experience and its lessons, just before the *Lord's Prayer*, come two teachings about service. The first is the parable of the Good Samaritan, wherein Jesus explains to the lawyer that loving one's neighbor is not about cataloguing which kind of person is worthy of his attention, but of responding to someone in need (10:25–37). The story-behind-the-story is that Jesus is the true 'Good Samaritan,' the despised outsider who paid the full price to redeem all victims of oppression, be it from the outside or from their own sin. He 'showed mercy,' thus bringing the greatest gift into the world of victims. The lawyer's eyes needed to be opened to true religion, which looks for people in need and (often anonymously) acts to love them through the power of Jesus Christ. It's a different world from the world of legalism and ritual.

[5] Francis Schaeffer, *True Spirituality*, Wheaton: Tyndale house, 1971, 42. Today, we might have used the terms 'propositional truth' and 'brute facts' differently. For Schaeffer, who was opposing theological liberalism, with its tendency to reduce the supernatural to myth, he is trying to say that heaven is a real place. Understanding the relation of the 'third heaven' to Paradise is the subject of much debate. For a helpful guide through the literature, see, Philip E. Hughes, *Commentary on the Second Epistle to the Corinthians*, Grand Rapids: Eerdmans, 1962, 428–439.

The second teaching comes from a simple meal in Bethany at the house of Martha, whose family was close to Jesus (10:38–42). While her sister Mary took advantage of the presence of the Lord and sat at his feet listening to his teaching, Martha was 'distracted by much serving.' When she complained to Jesus that she was left alone to serve, he gently rebuked her and said she was 'anxious and troubled about many things,' whereas only one thing really matters. Using a play on words, he tells her that Mary has chosen the good portion (the word means a part, or a share, but can imply a portion of food at table). Mary, then, had chosen the right 'dish,' which was the once-in-a-lifetime opportunity to sit and learn from Jesus. Modern readers often sympathize with Martha, who obeyed the rules of etiquette in the Near East rather than neglecting her duties, as she accused Mary of doing. But the text makes clear that there are times when priorities should change, because the Lord is in the house. When we seek first the Kingdom of God, somehow the rest will be provided (Matt. 6:33; Mark 10:28–31). Once again, here, Mary had eyes to see, while Martha was bound up in understandable, but enslaving anxieties.

Luke's version of the *Lord's Prayer* is given us in this context. Provoked by the example of Jesus 'praying in a certain place,' and by John the Baptist having taught his disciples to pray, one of the disciples asked Jesus to teach them how to pray. While it may appear that the writer mixes things together in a random patchwork, the flow is deliberate. If they could only see, if only they understood the kind of God we have, they would attain the greatest good. Effectiveness in missions is important, but compared to that, having eternal life in the knowledge of God is tantamount. Having a proper understanding of neighborly responsibility is good, but having a heart for victims, as does the Lord, is far better. Serving meals with proper diligence is good, but learning from Jesus is better. The *Lord's Prayer* as we find it here says the same thing. Regular prayer that is rightly formulated is good. Blessing the Father, desiring his Kingdom, looking for his provision and the forgiveness of sins, releasing others from debts, and asking for fewer trials, those are better.

They are better because they see the world right side up. The fallen world where so many things are broken, and where a worldview of vain attempts to succeed purely by human effort have so often replaced the true perspective where God needs to intervene if we are going to find solace. Only those who have eyes to see it can say the prayer sincerely. The ensuing teaching confirms it. If we ask insistently, if we seek by knocking hard on the door, even in the middle of the night, God will answer (11:5-13). Unlike the reluctant friend, God is a Father who cannot refuse any good thing to his children. Indeed, he cannot refuse to give his children the very best thing, his Holy Spirit (v. 13). If we only knew 'what kind of love the Father has given us' (1 John 3:1) we would order our priorities according to his, and it would show in our prayers. So often, instead, we pray and live as though God did not need to exist, as though a bit of good human effort could get us through, as though normal economic life locked us in to the world's system.

First century Jewish background

Although evidence is not as clear as we might like, the *Lord's Prayer* is not isolated from the immediate context in which Our Lord lived and taught. There are several parallels between this prayer and the prayers of the synagogue. For example, the famous *Qaddish* (Holy), the ancient Aramaic prayer used at the close of the main portion of the liturgy, while resolutely Jewish, nevertheless is quite close to much that is in the *Lord's Prayer*:

> May the great Name of God be exalted and sanctified, throughout the world, which he has created according to his will.

> May his Kingship be established in your lifetime and in your days, and in the lifetime of the entire household of Israel, swiftly and in the near future; and say, Amen.

> May his great name be blessed, forever and ever. Blessed, praised, glorified, exalted, extolled, honored, elevated and lauded be the Name of the holy one.

> Blessed is he—above and beyond any blessings and hymns, praises and consolations which are uttered in the world; and say Amen.

> May there be abundant peace from Heaven, and life, upon us and upon all Israel; and say, Amen.

One cannot miss the similarities to the prayer Jesus taught his disciples. The main thrust of the *Qaddish* is the exalted name of God. God is to be sanctified. Also, his kingdom is to be established on earth. At the same time the *Qaddish* is less intimate. The God of the *Qaddish* is so far above the earth that he is 'beyond praises and consolations which are uttered in the world.' The kingdom should come, but soon, in our lifetime, and mainly for the Jews. But Jesus' prayer is more comprehensive. 'Your kingdom come, your will be done, on earth as it is in heaven,' while not lacking in immediacy, has a broader reach. And certain elements of the *Lord's Prayer* are not in the *Qaddish* at all, such as the forgiveness of sins and protection from evil.

The forgiveness of sins is found in other first-century prayers. For example, Sirach has, 'Forgive your neighbor the wrong he has done, and then your sins will be pardoned when you pray' (28:2). The Qumran Psalm Scroll contains a poem-like prayer, entitled, 'A Plea for Deliverance,' which includes this petition: 'Let not Satan rule over me nor an unclean spirit.' Qumran indeed has several texts that are similar to portions of the *Lord's Prayer*. For example, an apocryphal psalm contains this final request: 'Remember me and forget me not, and lead me not into situations too hard for me.'[6]

---

[6] See, Simon Kistemaaker, 'The Lord's Prayer in the First Century,' *Journal of the Evangelical Theological Society* 21/4, Dec., 1978, 325.

Such parallels, with their differences, should come as no surprise. The Christian religion was born in a specifically first century context, even though its teachings are universal and for all times. When one is familiar with this setting (including what is called Second Temple Judaism) we can easily see a number of equivalent expressions of the spirituality practiced. At the same time, it is striking how Jesus' teaching is far more radical than any of the comparable texts. No wonder that upon hearing the Sermon on the Mount, the assembled crowds were astonished at his teaching, and recognized his far greater authority than that of the religious leaders of the day (Matt. 7:28–29).

Furthermore, the Gospels reaffirm every component of the *Lord's Prayer*. God is called Father in heaven (a phrase used 23 times in Matthew, and there are parallels in places like Mark 11:25; Luke 10:21; John 17:10). God is to be worshiped. As we will see later, Jesus resists the devil's temptation in the desert by quoting Deuteronomy to show that God alone is to be worshiped (Matt. 4:10; Luke 4:8); John redirects human worship toward God alone, in nine different references. God's kingdom is to be sought (Matt. 6:33; Luke 21:31) and his will be done ('if anyone's will is to do God's will...' John 7:17; 'not my will, but yours...' Luke 22:42). His provision is asked for (consider the miracle of the multiplication of the loaves). Our sins need forgiving (Matt. 26:28; Mark 1:4; Luke 1:77; 24:47). We are urged to forgive the sins of others (Luke 17:4; John 20:23). And we plead for strength in the face of temptation, and for freedom from evil or the evil one (Matt. 18:7; Luke 22:46; John 17:15).

Thus, the theology, or worldview, represented in the *Lord's Prayer* is woven into the warp and woof of all of Jesus' teaching, and, indeed, in the doctrine found throughout the entire New Testament. No wonder, then, that the church has consistently said the *Prayer* and drawn from its instruction down the generations. No wonder the prayer has been a part of the catechisms of the church from the earliest times right down to the present. Having said that, though, we should never forget that this text is first and foremost not a catechism but a prayer. Like the *Qaddish* it has a doxology. But unlike the *Qaddish* the *Lord's Prayer* is spoken by those who lift up their souls into the hands of the one God who can answer, and in so doing, gives meaning to our entire lives. Like the center of an hourglass, the *Prayer* wonderfully concentrates all our longings, all our hopes and fears, all our needs, into a very few petitions, the bare necessities for human life.

Prayer

Be thou my vision, O Lord of my heart,
Be all else but naught to me, save that thou art;
Thou my best thought in the day and the night,
Both waking and sleeping, thy presence my light.

Be thou my wisdom, be thou my true word,
Be thou ever with me, and I with thee Lord;
Be thou my great Father, and I thy true son;
Be thou in me dwelling, and I with thee one.

Be thou my breastplate, my sword for the fight;
Be thou my whole armor, be thou my true might;
Be thou my soul's shelter, be thou my strong tower:
O raise thou me heavenward, great Power of my power.

Riches I heed not, nor man's empty praise:
Be thou mine inheritance now and always;
Be thou and thou only the first in my heart;
O Sovereign of Heaven, my treasure thou art.

High King of Heaven, thou Heaven's bright sun,
O grant me its joys after victory is won;
Great heart of my own heart, whatever befall,
Still be thou my vision, O Ruler of all.

(Old Irish, Mary Elizabeth Byrne, transl., 1905)

3

Prayer and the Coming Kingdom

> The idea of the catholicity of the kingdom—the insistence
> that it is at work everywhere, always, and for all, rather than
> in some places, at some times, and for some people—is an
> integral part of Jesus' teaching from start to finish. (Robert
> Farrar Capon)

Many attempts have been made at finding an overall rationale,
a meta-narrative to explain the *Lord's Prayer*. Donald Shriver
sees it as the ultimate counter-cultural statement against any
claim upon our lives that pretends to be above God. 'One could
speak of the Lord's Prayer, and especially its opening section,
therefore, as the ground of the early church's resistance to
politicized authority.[1] Indeed, one major challenge for the
Christian church in the first three centuries was the social
obligation in the Roman Empire to declare that Caesar is
Lord. Christians would pay their taxes, refuse revolution, join

---

[1] Donald W. Shriver, Jr., *The Lord's Prayer: A Way of Life*, Atlanta: John Knox
Press, 1983, 48.

the military, but they could not in conscience say, 'Caesar is Lord,' since there is only one Lord, the Father in heaven whose name alone is hallowed. Praying for the kingdom to come means asking for liberty from human oppressors, be they governmental or even ecclesiastical. It is the triumph of human solidarity over provincial solidarity.[2]

This is an attractive idea for many reasons. There is a good bit in Jesus' teaching that is indeed counter-cultural. But perhaps it misses something much deeper about the Prayer, about prayer itself. Jacques Ellul, the brilliant French sociologist, tells us that the main point of prayer is not discourse, but 'a form of life, the life with God.'[3] Similarly, New York pastor and theologian Timothy Keller fully appreciates the way the *Lord's Prayer* is centered on banishing idols. But this can only be so if we first banish the idols in our hearts, where there should be room only for the overwhelming presence of God himself: 'Instead [of coming with nervous laundry lists], we should always say, in effect, "Lord, let me see your glory as I haven't before, let me be so ravished with your grace that worry and self-pity and anger and indifference melt away!"'[4] The *Lord's Prayer* includes the idea of freedom from idols, but it goes beyond that, to be satisfied with nothing less than intimacy with God himself.

There is another theory about the *Lord's Prayer* initiated, I believe, by N. T. Wright, and picked up by many others, which argues that it is a plea for a second exodus.[5] Wright claims that just as the first exodus was preceded by the longing of

---

[2] Ibid., 49–50.

[3] *Prayer and Modern Man*, op. cit., 49. The French title reveals the radical nature of prayer: *L'impossible prière*.

[4] Timothy Keller, 'Prayer and the Gospel' [http://www.redeemer.com/connect/prayer/prayer_and_the_gospel.html]

[5] N. T. Wright, *Into God's Presence: Prayer in the New Testament*, ed. R.L. Longenecker. 2001, Grand Rapids, Eerdmans, 132–54. See also, Brant Pitre, 'The Lord's Prayer and the New Exodus,' *Letter and Spirit* 2 (2006), 69–96.

an oppressed people, finally delivered by a powerful God and placed in a new land, so the *Lord's Prayer* expresses the hopes of a people in the Second Temple period, 'that is, as the prayer of the new wilderness wandering people.' He goes on to show how each of the petitions makes sense in the light of this recasting of the escape from Egypt, so often referred to by the prophets. The *Lord's Prayer* accordingly reveals what can be called a 'typological eschatology,' in which the events of the first Exodus establish a prototype for how God will save his people in the end-times.[6]

This idea is also very attractive and makes a good deal of sense. There is no question that much in the New Testament echoes the great exodus from Egypt and the establishment of a people suited for God's praise. The author of Hebrews draws the specific parallel between the revelation at Mount Sinai and the great church in the heavenly Jerusalem. My only caution would be not to see the prayer, nor, indeed, our life in these end times, so much as a liberation, an escape from slavery, but more as an ingathering, providing the constitution of a new people for his praise. In that sense the prayer is more of a normal part of the new life in the gospel than a fresh parting of the waves of the Red Sea. They are closely related, and surely it would be far from N. T. Wright's intention to overlook the reality of the present. And, certainly, we are a wandering people, a diaspora in need of a safe passage to the new heaven (1 Pet. 1:1; James 1:1). Yet that should not be so underscored as to minimize the accomplishment of salvation right now, including the life we have, first, before God in humble fellowship, and, second, in the Christian community. We would not want, by using an exodus model, unintentionally to relativize the great priority of worship, with which the prayer begins.

Do we need to have one, all-embracing theme that unifies the *Lord's Prayer*? Perhaps not. Surely, though, one of its

[6] N. T. Wright, *Into God's Presence*, 146.

guiding arguments is for the coming of the kingdom. The petition, 'Thy kingdom come, thy will be done,' is at the center, almost like the hub of a wheel, from which the spokes radiate. As theologian-missiologist Harvie Conn puts it, 'So Jesus teaches us how to pray in the new age. The heart of the prayer he taught us is the heart of his message and his mission—the coming of the kingdom. 'Thy kingdom come,' he says. And in connection with that kingdom's coming, may the name of God be hallowed, may the will of God be done (Matt. 6:33; 5:19, 20). May there be a realization here and now of the saving gifts and blessings of God—forgiveness of sins (Jer. 31:34; Matt. 18:23ff.) and bread 'for the coming day.' May there be preservation from the apostasy of the last terrible hour of temptation, present now (John 16:33) but still to come in its fullest sense. For all these things, the followers of Jesus are to seek, to ask, to find (11:9ff.). And they will not be disappointed.'[7]

Today we rarely think about kingdoms or monarchies with any sense that they are still viable. For many modern people a kingdom will seem removed, almost like a land in a fairy-story. Of course, we know that various countries are ruled by kings (Morocco, Saudi Arabia, the United Arab Emirites are kingdoms, and the world also knows of many constitutional monarchies, where to one degree or another the royalty or the principality take part in the affairs of the people). But we are so used to thinking of government and societal values in terms of democracy, or socialism, or other bureaucratic forms that it requires some adjustment to put ourselves in the place of the first-century Jews who were looking to the coming of the great King. After all, Jesus did not proclaim 'the democratic republic of God is at hand!' The fact is, the coming of the kingdom is not only most important for *Lord's Prayer*, but is at the very heart of Jesus' message.

---

[7] Harvie M. Conn, 'Luke's Theology of Prayer,' *Christianity Today*, Dec. 22, 1972, 7–8.

Many commentators have drawn attention to the centrality of the kingdom of God in Jesus' preaching. Although he certainly preached on other themes, the presence of the kingdom of God is indeed the most often emphasized subject in his message. At the very beginning of his ministry, the Gospel writers set the scene: 'From that time Jesus began to preach, saying, "Repent, for the kingdom of heaven is at hand"' (Matt. 4:17; Mark 1:14). All first-hand accounts of the person and work of Christ presuppose this overarching theme. (For that matter, as we shall see, it is true for the apostle Paul as well.) When Mary knew she was to bear the Messiah, her prayer (known as the *Magnificat*, recorded in Luke 1:46–55) begins by acknowledging the honor that has been bestowed on her, but quickly moves to proclaim the power of God, and his mercy to every generation of those who fear him.

> He has shown strength with his arm;
>> He has scattered the proud in the thoughts of their hearts;
> He has brought down the mighty from their thrones
>> And exalted those of humble estate;
> He has filled the hungry with good things,
>> And the rich he has sent away empty (vv. 51–53).

Mary draws on an earlier prayer by Hannah (1 Sam. 2:1–10). Hannah had been unable to bear a child to the husband who loved her. She had prayed fervently for a son whom she could dedicate for priestly service. At the right time, in his perfect timing, the Lord answered this dear woman. Hannah's son turned out to be none other than Samuel, who became the greatest judge in Israel, who kept the Philistines at bay, and paved the way for the reorganization of Israel into a kingdom. Mary's son was none other than Jesus, a greater Samuel, who would defeat all of God's enemies, and inaugurate the era of the kingdom of God. Mary recognized the parallel to her own situation, and adapted this prayer of thanks to the miraculous conception of Christ.

The kingdom in the Old Testament

We do not find the expression 'kingdom of heaven' in so many words in the Old Testament, and only rarely is the word kingdom joined in a phrase directly to God (as, for example, in Psalm 45:6, or Daniel 5:21). Yet of course they are there by implication. At the dawn of creation, mankind was made after God's own image, and charged with several great tasks, or callings. Humans were to be fruitful and multiply, and fill the earth. They were to labor over it (Gen. 1:28–30, 2:5, 15). These ordinances are sometimes known as the 'cultural mandate.' If, for the sake of argument, we define culture as *cultivation* in the broadest sense, not only tilling the earth, but moving about the creation to discover and develop its potential in every area of life, then these callings are abundant and fulfilling indeed.

However, first, and most important, human beings were to worship the Lord their maker. The author of Genesis is concise, but we can find this central vocation stated in the earliest chapters both by implication and more directly. Human beings were made vice-gerunds, rulers over God's creation, but always under his greater Lordship. Indeed, the image of God leads directly to one of our chief characteristics: we are kings under the great King. The Sabbath was given to mankind, modeled on God's own rest from his labors in the creation of the world. As we rest from our own labors, it is appropriate to contemplate the goodness of God our King in worship. When the Lord forbade our first parents from partaking of the tree of the knowledge of good and evil, he was not exercising capricious jealousy, but his divine right to set limits for his creatures.

Throughout the Old and New Testaments, it is made abundantly clear that our primary purpose is to worship the King of Kings and Lord of Lords (Ps. 136:3; 1 Tim. 6:15; Rev. 17:14, 19:16). The thought is made wonderfully clear in the first question and answer to the *Westminster Shorter Catechism*: Q. What is the chief end of man? A. Man's chief end is to glorify God, and enjoy him forever. Note the order. First to glorify God, then to enjoy him forever. Despite attempts to meld the two by saying we can glorify God *by* enjoying him, the Divines who penned these words knew better. Joy, for them, is not happiness or pleasure, but the profound privilege of those captured by God's honor. The Middle English, *joy*, as well as the Anglo-French, *joie*, derive from the Latin *gaudēre* (to be glad), and possibly from the Greek *gēthein* (to rejoice). These are comprehensive terms, meaning that our enjoyment of something or someone is a most fulfilling experience. Enjoyment of God is, then, the most fulfilling experience we could have. It means satisfaction with God, contentment with him, whether or not we may feel altogether happy at a particular time. God is the kind of King who always knows what is best for his subjects, without having to ask them or check-in with them.

Because of the fall into sin and misery, however, this marvelous vocation was lost, and related callings marred. Would the Lord leave mankind in misery, ending in death? He could have done so, with full justice. Yet, wonderfully, he had mercy on his creatures and provided a way of restoration. Indeed, he provided a way beyond restoration, to new measures of grace with joy. Through the defeat of the serpent, the 'death of death,' God would begin to remake the world. The King would provide a new kingdom, not corrupted by sin.

A distinction can be observed between two, related, kinds of manifestations of the kingdom in the Old Testament. The first is the celebration of God's power and dominion over all the creation. 'Great are the works of the Lord, studied by all who delight in them. Full of splendor and majesty is his work, and his righteousness endures forever' (Ps. 111:2–3). 'Have you not known? Have you not heard? The Lord is the everlasting God, the Creator of the ends of the earth' (Isa. 40:28).

The second is his rule over Israel in particular. As Israel's national power declined, she increasingly emphasized the reality of God's kingly victory over her enemies in the future. And increasingly that victory is associated with the Messiah. In Daniel's prophecies this hope is quite explicit. Consider the great discourse about the Son of Man in which the earthly kingdoms are shown to fail:

> But the court shall sit in judgment,
>> And [the fourth beast's] dominion shall be taken away,
>> to be consumed and destroyed to the end.
> And the kingdom and the dominion
>> and the greatness of the kingdoms under the whole heaven
>> shall be given to the people of the saints of the Most High;
> their kingdom shall be an everlasting kingdom,
>> and all dominions shall serve and obey him (Dan. 7:27).

The more Israel's identity and rule were threatened by her enemies, the more extravagant were the pledges of its future rule. Particularly in the minor prophets, we find promises to Israel of the coming of an astonishing realm where the knowledge and joy of the Lord fills the people of the earth.

> And on that day there shall be inscribed on the bells of the horses, 'Holy to the Lord.' And the pots in the house of the Lord shall be as the bowls before the altar. And every pot in Jerusalem and Judah shall be holy to the Lord (Zech. 14:20–21).

Whereas the shape of many of these promises is in terms of the restoration of Israel, the content often bursts out of that shape, and refers to a 'higher, spiritual and imperishable reality.'[8] All comes to a head with the *Day of the Lord*, when the wicked shall be judged and the oppressed people of the Lord will be delivered. An entirely new dispensation is foretold (Hosea 4:3; Isa. 2:10ff.). The salvation to come cannot perish, death shall be

---

[8] Herman Ridderbos, *The Coming of the Kingdom*, Philadelphia: Presbyterian & Reformed, 1962, 5.

defeated, and a new heaven and a new earth shall be established (Isa. 60:19; 65:17; 66:22, etc.).

From our vantage point twenty one centuries later we easily lose sight of the anticipation and excitement surrounding the events of the first century, recorded in the New Testament. When Mark records Jesus' opening words that the kingdom is at hand, he adds: 'The time is fulfilled' (1:15). This is the long awaited era of fulfillment, when Jesus Christ comes to reveal all of the glory of God. The former times, Paul tells us, were times of slavery to elemental principles. 'But when the fullness of time had come, God sent forth his Son, born of woman, born under the law, to redeem those who were under the law...' (Gal. 4:4). Thus, when he teaches his followers to pray, 'thy kingdom come,' he is drawing them in to this momentous era, where every priority is wrapped up in this kingdom.

The character of the kingdom

What, then, are the chief characteristics of this kingdom, that we should see it at the center of our concerns? We shall have more to say about the details when we come to this particular petition. But for now, suffice it to say the kingdom is first and foremost God-centered. Christ, the Second Person of the Trinity become flesh, is the very embodiment of the kingdom's nature and purpose. He is the long awaited king. This God-centered meaning is at the very heart of his preaching, and then of his death and resurrection. The first three petitions of the *Lord's Prayer* make it clear that he wants this to be inscribed in our thoughts and identity. As Ridderbos comments:

> In the first petition the meaning of the coming of the kingdom is described as the effectual inducement of man to do homage to God's virtues ('hallowing his name'). And in accordance with this is the carrying out of his revealed will on earth as it is now done in heaven. The coming of the kingdom is first of all the display of the divine glory, the

re-assertion and maintenance of God's rights on earth in their full sense.[9]

The kingdom is not primarily a realm of activity, although wherever it is established great goings on do occur. It does not come by a steady, gradual evolution, although one can expect progress when the kingdom is received. Rather, it is God's breaking through, his 'rending the heavens,' with fire and quaking mountains, something no one had ever heard nor seen till now (Isa. 64:1-4).

Previously the God-centered kingdom had come in many phases, and in many parts of history. Finally, however, with the coming of Jesus Christ, it arrives in its ultimate form. For we are in the end times. Paul explains this to the Galatians, comparing the former times to childhood: 'But when the fullness of time had come, God sent forth his Son, born of a woman, under the law, to redeem those who were under the law...' (Gal. 4:4). History, always under God's control, now comes to a climax. Putting it one way, there are no more major events to take place since Jesus is here and rules the world as the risen Christ. That is why Paul calls the Corinthians, and us by association, those 'on whom the end of the ages has come' (1 Cor. 10:11).

To be sure, we await the final judgment and the entrance into heaven or hell. Jesus is coming again, this time not to deal with sin, since that has already been accomplished (Heb. 9:27-28). Rather it is to finish up what he has already begun to do in gathering his people. An imperfect parallel can be made to the invasion of the Normandy beaches at D-Day and the rest of the war. When those beaches had been secured, June 6, 1944, it became only a matter of time until the final defeat of the Nazis across Europe. The parallel is not exact since Jesus' victory on the cross was unique, and the application of redemption which follows is dependent on that finished work in a way the allied

[9] *The Coming of the Kingdom*, op. cit., 20-21.

armies were not exactly continually drawing upon Normandy. Still, the effect of Christ's death and resurrection was to secure, once and for all, the land that had gone astray. We now await the final judgment and the entrance into the new heavens, which is the 'not-yet' of the formula, 'already-not-yet.'

The kingdom brings God's judgment to earth. At last, his glory is revealed, and he is vindicated. Judgment occurs in two phases. First, the sins of his people are judged at the cross of Christ. Calvary is indeed a judgment, but visited not on God's people, as they deserve, but on the beloved Son, who takes their place. Second, God's will is done over against those set on resisting him. The terrible day of judgment means all his enemies will perish. Revelation 18 is an extended recitation of the power, the thoroughness and the injuries inflicted on every individual and every society pitting themselves against God. Both of these judgments have an 'already-not-yet' characteristic. While Jesus' death was his finished work, and all believers are 'buried with him by baptism into death (Rom. 6:3), yet the judgment of the 'great white throne' will reveal in a final way who's names are written in the book of life (Rev. 20:11). And while God's judgments are already abroad, and the axe is laid to the foot of the tree (Matt. 3:10; Luke 3:9), the final judgment is not until the very last day, at the end of all history.

Lest the thought of judgment terrify us, we need remember that Jesus Christ came to reveal the loving character of his Father. The coming of the kingdom in the New Testament is fundamentally a story about the grace of God to undeserving people. Still, that grace proffered on his people was immeasurably costly because of the price Jesus paid. He endured God's judgment for his people. And on the last day, we shall fully observe the cost for unbelievers who have denied God, as he banishes them from his sight. The heart of the kingdom, then, is the gospel of salvation, followed by the finality of the last judgment.

For now, in the time of God's patience, the coming of the kingdom is primarily in the power to change lives and cultures.

And that power is found in and through Jesus Christ. When the angel told Joseph to take Mary as his wife, he explained that their child's name would be Jesus, 'for he will save his people from their sins' (Matt. 1:21). Similarly, Zechariah prophesied that his son, John the Baptist, would prepare the way for the Lord to come who would 'give knowledge of salvation to his people in the forgiveness of their sins, because of the tender mercy of God' (Luke 1:77-78). This free gift comes with certain demands. While the Bible carefully teaches the difference between the gift and the demand, the church often forgets the difference. Salvation is a gift, with no conditions attached to receiving it by faith. Yet believers who do embrace the gift are changed forever, and they will want to walk in the light of God's high demands.

For Jesus, the gift and the command are not confused. This is why the Sermon on the Mount begins with the *Beatitudes*, not the retelling of the law. One can see this simply in the way he proclaimed the forgiveness of sins. He always did so based on his own authority. For example in the story of the paralytic lowered through the roof, Jesus states boldly, 'My son, your sins are forgiven' (Mark 2:5). His critics did not miss the significance of this declaration. Only God can forgive sins. But Jesus came as the Messiah, the Son of Man whose mission is to bring salvation to his people.

At the same time, the gospel is comprehensive. While the priority should always be kept straight, forgiveness is always a freely given divine endowment, it is not narrowly about removing guilt, with no other consequences. We see this clearly in the story of the paralytic just mentioned. Because in the sequel, Jesus replies to his critics that it is no easier to forgive sins than to heal the man on the stretcher. So he told him to rise up and carry his bed home. Only God could do either of these. And God does both, he forgives, and he heals. By this act of healing, his listeners would know that 'the Son of Man has authority on earth to forgive sins' (Mark 2:10).

This is why in his first sermon at the synagogue in Nazareth, he could quote Isaiah to the effect that the Spirit of the Lord was upon him to proclaim good news to the poor, liberty to the captives, healing for the blind and freedom for the oppressed (Luke 4:18, from Isa. 61:1-2). The great year of Jubilee has broken in, because Jesus has arrived. Again, although at first his audience was glad to hear this, when they listened more closely they realized that they were the oppressors, refusing to help the poor and the diseased. Indeed, this passage from Isaiah was a condemnation of the religious system that had stifled the real gospel. Thus, they tried to get rid of Jesus (Luke 4:20-30).

The gospel of salvation at the center of the kingdom of heaven is thus holistic. While it is appropriate to separate between faith and works, they ultimately must go together. The apostle Paul declares to the Romans that he is not ashamed of the gospel, 'for it is the power of God for salvation to everyone who believes, to the Jew first and also to the Greek' (Rom. 1:16). Again, this gospel is comprehensive. Notice the full context: 'for in it the righteousness of God is revealed from faith to faith' (v. 17). God's righteousness is not simply to sensitize us to praying or going to church. Nor is it uniquely a moral renovation. His righteousness covers every area of life from the love of God to the love of neighbor. To put it in Abraham Kuyper's terms, 'In the total expanse of human life there is not a single square inch of which the Christ, who alone is sovereign, does not declare, "That is mine!"' Perhaps because we so often hear in the appeals of preachers only the offer of entering heaven in the afterlife, we have got it in our heads that salvation is merely of the individual soul.

To be sure, there are other loci besides the kingdom for the truth of Jesus' teaching and work as well as what the New Testament is all about. Think of justification by faith, or the final manifestation of the covenant. Yet no one locus of truth is quite as comprehensive as the kingdom. Such realities as the covenant, for example, or justification through faith, these are certainly a most important part of the kingdom. But, to quote Ridderbos again, 'The idea of the kingdom of God is more comprehensive [than even justification or covenant] exactly because it is not only oriented to the redemption of God's people, but to the self-assertion of God in *all* his works.[10]

The kingdom and the church

This is not the place for an extensive treatment of the relationship between the kingdom and the church.[11] The *Lord's Prayer* is clearly meant to be prayed by the church of Jesus Christ. The prayer was given to the disciples. The petitions are all plural: 'give *us* this day,' 'forgive *us* our debts,' 'lead *us* not,' etc. Nothing forbids saying this prayer individually, but the thrust of it is clearly for the community.

That the term *ecclesia* (the church, the 'called-out ones') is only found in two verses in the Gospels, both in Matthew (16:18; 17:18), should not mislead us into thinking that little in Jesus' preaching concerns the church. These two texts are important because they describe the unassailable authority of the church together with instructions on the discipline of the gathered community. But just about everything Jesus said and did was in view of gathering a people for the covenant relation, where God is our God and we are his people. Jesus is the Messiah, and the entire purpose of God's anointed one is to assemble a people for himself. The very central message of the kingdom, the gospel of salvation, is primarily directed at people, Christ's people. The kingdom can be entered, it can be purged, its message preached to the nations. Just as many in the Israel of the Old Testament lost sight of the gospel, so now,

---

[10] *The Coming of the Kingdom*, op. cit., 23.

[11] See R. T. France, 'The Church and the Kingdom of God,' *Biblical Interpretation and the Church: Text and Context*, D. A. Carson, ed., Exeter: Paternoster, 1984, 30–44; George Eldon Ladd, *A Theology of the New Testament*, Eerdmans, 1974, 111–119.

in the New Testament the gospel is received by many renewed persons, both Jews and Gentiles.

So the two are very close. Geerhardus Vos puts it this way: 'The church is a form which the kingdom assumes in result of the new stage upon which the Messiahship of Jesus enters with his death and resurrection.'[12] He sees the invisible church and kingdom membership as virtually synonymous. Yet Vos adds that with regard to the visible church there is a difference. While the visible church is one important outward expression of the invisible kingdom, it is not the only one.

> Undoubtedly the kingship of God, as his recognized and applied supremacy, is intended to pervade and control the whole of human life in all its forms of existence, this the parable of the leaven plainly teaches. These various forms of human life have their own sphere in which they work and embody themselves. There is a sphere of science, a sphere of art, a sphere of the family and of the state, a sphere of commerce and industry. Whenever one of these spheres comes under the controlling influence of the principle of the divine supremacy and glory, and this outwardly reveals itself, there can we truly say that the kingdom of God has become manifest.[13]

Here, Vos is drawing on the thought of Abraham Kuyper (1837–1920) who developed the notion of 'sphere sovereignty,' the rule of Christ over every area of human life. Though Vos does not elaborate on the role of common grace, nor does he discuss exactly what this 'controlling influence' might look like, he does say that these different spheres, no less than the

[12] Geerhardus Vos, *The Kingdom and the Church*, Phillipsburg: P & R Publishers, 1979, 86.
[13] Ibid., 87–88.

visible church, come under the sway of the kingdom of God because of the regenerating work of the Holy Spirit.[14]

Again, following Ridderbos, we can say, the *kingdom* is the great divine work of salvation in its fulfillment and consummation in Christ; whereas the *church* is the people elected and called by God and sharing in the bliss of the kingdom.[15] In the midst of this bliss is everything the *Prayer* tells us. We worship God, whom we call our Father. We focus all of life on him and the coming of his kingdom. We want his will to be done in every aspect of life. We utterly depend on him for food and raiment and everything needful. We desperately need him to forgive our sins, and to give us the grace to forgive others. Without his protection we will be thrown to the wolves and tested beyond our capacity to resist.

Thus, when we pray the *Lord's Prayer*, with its central petition, 'thy kingdom come, thy will be done, on earth as it is in heaven,' we are asking God to continue to break through and transform all of human life. We are asking that God's will be done here on earth, because it is not yet being fully and perfectly done as it is in God's own dwelling, surrounded by the angels. In short, we are asking that this great reforming power, by the authority of Jesus the Messiah, come and affect every area of life, from our guilt and pollution, to the relief of the oppressed, and to our safekeeping until we see the Lord face-to-face in uninterrupted glory.

[14] Ibid., 88–89.
[15] *The Coming of the Kingdom.* Op. cit., 354.

Hymn

Jesus shall reign where'er the sun
does its successive journeys run;
his kingdom spread from shore to shore,
till moons shall wax and wane no more.

To Jesus endless prayer be made,
and endless praises crown his head;
his name like sweet perfume shall rise
with every morning sacrifice.

People and realms of every tongue
dwell on his love with sweetest song;
and infant voices shall proclaim
their early blessings on his name.

Blessings abound where'er he reigns;
all prisoners leap and loose their chains;
the weary find eternal rest,
and all who suffer want are blest.

Let every creature rise and bring
honors peculiar to our King;
angels descend with songs again,
and earth repeat the loud amen!

(Isaac Watts, 1719)

4

Our Father Who Art in Heaven, Hallowed Be Thy Name

The dramatic person could not tread the stage unless he concealed a real person: unless the real and unknown I existed, I would not even make mistakes about the imagined me. And in prayer this real I struggles to speak, for once, from his real being, and to address, for once, not the other actors, but—what shall I call Him? The Author, for He invented us all? The Producer, for he controls all? Or the audience, for he watches, and will judge the performance? (C. S. Lewis)

Names matter a great deal in the Bible, and in the ancient world, much more than they do in the modern West. Abraham means father of a multitude. Isaac means laughter (first, from the skeptical reaction of his ninety-year old mother upon hearing the prediction that she would again carry a child, then from the joy of his birth). Saul was met on the Damascus road by the living Christ, and then began to live, not as a persecutor of the church, but as its greatest builder. As so, beginning with his first missionary journey, he was more often known by his

Roman name, Paul, presumably because it would give him better access to the Gentiles (Acts 13:9). The Lord gave Peter, or Cephas, a name change, no doubt in part because of his character, but also because of his key role at the founding of the Christian church (John 1:42; see Matt. 16:18). All believers will be given a *new* name written on a white stone. Possibly a reference to the way ancient courts cast votes, the white stone meant acquittal, the black one meant guilt (Rev. 2:17).

And of course the name of God is particularly significant. The Old Testament identifies God with several names. *Elohim* means God in his grandeur, or the God of gods. *El Shaddai* means God Almighty. *Adonai* means God the Master. There are other names. The most often used name is the *tetragrammaton*, or four Hebrew letters, YHWH. Given to Moses in Exodus 3:13–15, by the time it came down in the Hebrew manuscripts the vowels had been forgotten, because of the Jewish belief that one should not pronounce the name of God, believing it to be too sacred even to utter. So different vowels have been suggested, yielding Yahweh, or Jehovah. Most often translators simply render the word 'The Lord,' sometimes using capitals. To forbid even pronouncing God's name stemmed from a legalistic superstition. Yet it is true that the Bible everywhere tells us to respect the name of God, and never to take that name in vain. This can be done by swearing, of course, but it is much deeper than bad language to take God's name in vain. We can make vows in the name of God, as we might at a wedding, and then break them. We can even give God a 'bad name' before others by our poor comportment. Ironically, the Pharisees seemed to use God's name far too casually when they formulated their oaths, so Jesus put strict limits on formulating them (Matt. 5:33–37).

Our Father

Thus the opening statement of the *Lord's Prayer* is a bold and personal declaration. To whom are our prayers addressed? To a heavenly Father. God is our Father. What an extraordinary thought! The notion is not entirely new. When Moses stood before Pharaoh he was to declare, 'Thus says the Lord, "Israel is my firstborn son...let my son go..."' (Ex. 4:22–23). When the later apostasy of the same people was foreseen, the Lord asks them why they are ungrateful, because, 'Is not he your Father who created you...?' (Deut. 32:6). When God made his covenant with David, he promised that he would be a Father to David's offspring, and though he would discipline him when he went astray, he would never withdraw his steadfast love from him (2 Sam. 14–15). Psalm 68:5 calls God the 'Father of the fatherless.' Psalm 89:26 puts it in the context of prayer: 'He shall cry to me, "You are my Father, my God, and the Rock of my salvation".'

When the prophets predict the deliverance of Israel, and of the Gentiles, they several times describe his new people as entering into his family. Isaiah prays poignantly for mercy:

> Look down from heaven and see,
>> From your holy and beautiful habitation.
> Where are your zeal and your might?
>> The stirring of your inner parts and your compassion
>> are held back from me.
> For you are our Father,
>> Though Abraham does not know us,
>> And Israel does not acknowledge us;
> You, O Lord, are our Father,
>> Our Redeemer from of old is your name (Isa. 63:15–16).

Still, the identification of God as Father is relatively rare in the Old Testament.

The New Testament, however, speaks often about God's fatherhood. Jesus called him Father in a special sense. His critics recognized that the way he called God his own Father amounted to claiming he himself was equal to God (John 5:18). And they were right. Indeed, Jesus derived his earthly authority from his unique relationship with his Father (John 5:19–24).

But most significantly, he also identified God as *our* Father. In the Sermon itself Jesus calls God 'our Father' or 'your Father' seventeen times. In Matthew's Gospel Jesus calls God the Father of his people over and over. It is the same in the rest of the Gospels, and particularly in John's Gospel. Paul's calling God the Father is especially poignant in that he focuses on the grace of adoption. So does John, particularly in his first letter. John exclaims, 'See what kind of love the Father has given to us, that we should be called the children of God; and so we are' (1 John 3:1). Commenting on our adoption, The *Westminster Confession of Faith* talks about our liberties and privileges, being able to call God *Abba*, Father, receiving pity, protection, provisions, being chastened but never cast off (WCF XII).[1] A new consciousness is therefore upon the disciples, and upon us. God is a Father to us.

More than this, the heart of our covenant relationship with God is for him to 'put his name' on his people. The marvelous three-fold blessing established by Aaron is this (Num. 6:24–26):

> The Lord bless you and keep you;
> The Lord make his face to shine upon you and be gracious to you;
> The Lord lift up his countenance upon you and give you peace.

That is the blessing (v. 23). But here is how it is confirmed: 'So they shall put my name upon the people of Israel, and I will bless them' (v. 27). God's very name is put upon his people! The Hebrew word *suwm* means to place, to set, to establish—so by placing his name upon his people God is establishing them in their identity. They are *his*, but he is *theirs*.

---

[1] There has been a good deal of scholarly discussion about the meaning of 'Abba.' For years it was thought to be a child-like name, resembling 'Daddy.' That has been pretty much dismissed. In the three uses of the word in the New Testament, it is always in conjunction with 'the Father' (Mark 14:36; Rom. 8:15; Gal. 4:6). Thus, Abba, the Father, probably means to say, 'Abba, as we say it in Aramaic, that is, the Father.'

After a period of testing and refining, the prophet Zechariah tells the people, 'They will call upon my name, and I will answer them. I will say, "They are my people"; and they will say, "The Lord [YHWH] is my God [Elohim]"' (Zech. 13:9). So, God's naming of us, and our naming the name of God is the very heart of our faith. God is our dwelling place from everlasting to everlasting (Ps. 90:1). And now he puts his name on us as we call upon his name. The *Lord's Prayer*, then, is the fulfillment of this promise. Whenever we pray, 'Our Father, who art in heaven,' we are calling upon his name. When he answers, he is naming us after himself.

But it gets even better. Because in the New Testament God's name is fully revealed in Jesus Christ. The Second Person of the divine Trinity became a man, the 'God-man,' to use Anselm's expression. His name is the most excellent name of all, far superior even to those of angels (Heb. 1:4; Phil. 2:9). We now do all things in Christ's name (Eph. 5:20; cf. 3:17). But, astonishingly, it works the other way. Most significantly, we who are believers are called *Christ*-ians (Acts 11:26; 26:28). We may suffer as Christians, but we will always be delivered (1 Pet. 4:16). Naming the name is at once a privilege and a responsibility. We remember God's name alone because only his rule is just and peaceful (Isa. 26:13). Paul tells his readers through Timothy, 'Let everyone who names the name of the Lord depart from iniquity' (2 Tim. 2:19). But the victory is assured because he names us after his own name.

Earthly fathers

Certain people, when they hear that God is a Father, become understandably troubled. The reason is often that their own father was far from the kind, protective, provident Father in heaven of the *Prayer*. Although abusive fathers have always been around, we know today much more about this sad phenomenon. Abuse may be, and often is, physical. Inadequate fathers beat their children in their frustration and in their desire to be obeyed. We are not talking about the occasional slap on the backside after fair warning, in a home where discipline is consistent and joined to love. We are talking about the arbitrary violence applied to a victim unable to defend himself, herself, or even to hide. As we increasingly recognize, abuse can be verbal and emotional as well as physical. When a parent, or a boss, or any person in power, tells the child or other victim how inadequate they are, or embarrasses them in front of others, and that sort of thing, we have a kind of abuse that is, if possible, more difficult to recover from than physical abuse. This cruelty is far more widespread than we may think. I heard one family psychologist state that one out of every three women sitting in the pew of a typical church has been abused.

How do we explain to such victims that God is not like this? We can try to explain that any earthly analogy to God's nature is inadequate. God is the good shepherd, yet earthly shepherds are at times far from good at their work. God is our dwelling place, yet most earthly abodes are far from sufficient. God is enthroned forever, yet most earthly potentates are flawed and arbitrary. God is the bridegroom, yet most earthly husbands are far from adequate. Thus, when we call God our Father, we do so in the understanding that no earthly father can come close to the heavenly image. These earthly parallels are merely useful, if true, descriptions of qualities in God never approached by the earthly analogies. Even if one had a marvelous father on earth, he could never come close to the fatherhood of God.[2]

And many of us have had loving fathers. It would be a mistake to be so sensitive to victims of abuse that we forget that there are many good fathers, who would have done anything for us to ensure the wellbeing of their children. In my own case I had parents who sent me to the best schools, provided shelter and housing, and did all they could to teach me how to get along

---

[2] Some cases, especially where the damage is extensive, call for psychological counseling.

in society. When the Scripture compares God to a father it is generally to elicit the positive characteristics of our fathers. In Psalm 103 we are told, 'As a father shows compassion to his children, so the Lord shows compassion to his children' (v. 13). Jesus appeals to the image of a provident earthly father to argue that God the Father will provide for his children even better than they, as we mentioned in chapter one (Luke 11:11-13).

Still, even the best earthly father cannot come close to the true heavenly Father. So, whatever the case, where our own parents were good, or not good, or something between, we should look to the heavenly model as the standard for what ought to be on earth. 'Therefore, be imitators of God,' the apostle tells his Ephesian readers. Which then leads him to describe marriage, parenthood, and servitude in imitation of the higher model. So then, if we have had a substandard father, we can approach the Lord and learn what a true father can be, and then reevaluate our own case, sometimes taking appropriate measures to deal with it. And even if we have had a wonderful father, we can still approach the Lord and learn of the great source of excellent earthly fatherhood. Come, then, and know the true Father, the One who is in heaven, and is ever ready to care for you!

A number of confessional documents contain insightful, even beautiful portions on the doctrine of Adoption. The *Westminster Confession of Faith* devotes a rich paragraph to Adoption (chapter XII). It is worth quoting in full:

> All those that are justified, God vouchsafes, in and for His only Son Jesus Christ, to make partakers of the grace of adoption, by which they are taken into the number, and enjoy the liberties and privileges of the children of God, have His name put upon them, receive the spirit of adoption, have access to the throne of grace with boldness, are enabled to cry, Abba, Father, are pitied, protected, provided for, and chastened by Him as by a Father: yet never cast off, but sealed to the day of redemption; and inherit the promises, as heirs of everlasting salvation.

All these blessings are true for the believer, and the *Lord's Prayer* opens with the thankful acknowledgement of these truths.

Calling God our Father also brings to mind his divine Providence. By this term we refer to the Lord's government of the world in general and of his people in particular. Nothing is outside of his control, even the darker matters of life. God has made the world real, with human agency as significant. Thus, he does not guide us like the puppeteer, who pulls on strings to make the doll dance about. We have here the mystery of God's full sovereignty and yet the full responsibility of human action, a subject to which we shall return.

What is important to remember here, as we call upon God as Father, is his Fatherly goodness toward us. A verse we love to quote, and possibly can become casual about, is Romans 8:28: 'And we know that for all those who love God all things work together for good, for those who are called according to his purpose.' Notice the verse does not say, 'all things *are* good.' That might be true for Hinduism, where everything is lost in a sea of unity, but not for the Christian faith, where good and evil are absolutely and completely opposite. What Paul is telling us here is that every part of his Providence, even the darker parts, *work together* for the good. The French translation is helpful: 'everything is in *concert* for the good.' Like a great symphony, you could not play individual parts in isolation from the rest and have it make much sense. Just listening to the flutes, or the tympani alone would be jarring. But remove them from the full orchestration and it won't sound nearly as good.

Sinclair Ferguson comments in many of his writings and sermons on Providence. He likes to quote the Puritan John Flavel, who once remarked 'The Providence of God is like Hebrew words—it can be read only backwards.'[3] That is, we

---

[3] Quoted in Sinclair Ferguson, *In Christ Alone: Living the Gospel Centered Life*, Orlando: The Reformation Trust, 2007, 167. Quoted from Flavel's 'Navigation Spiritualized.'

often can only make sense of God's Providence in retrospect. Why are we not told more in advance? Dr. Ferguson suggests, '[Flavel's words] have reminded me to fix my mind and heart on God's wise, gracious, and sovereign rule, and on the assurance that he works everything together for His children's good, so that I do not inquire too proudly into why I cannot understand His sovereign purposes.'[4]

So, then, we have a Father who adopts us as children into his family, and then provides everything good for us. We know this for a certainty because, 'He who did not spare his own Son but gave him up for us all, how will he not also with him graciously give us all things? (Rom. 8:32).

In heaven

Why does the Lord name him our Father *in heaven*? Surely this points to his uniqueness as Father. God is not like earthly fathers, who may know how to give good things to their children but yet are so far from perfect (Matt. 7:11). He is the Father of lights (James 1:17). He is the Father of spirits (Heb. 12:9). He is the Father of glory (Eph. 1:17). Yet at the same time, as we can see from the rest of the prayer, God is not a distant deity. Donald W. Shriver, Jr., calls this 'the bond of tender supremacy.'[5]

Besides the greatness of God, the second presupposition of the *Lord's Prayer*, as it is throughout the Bible, is that we live in a fallen world. While still God's creation, and to be respected and enjoyed as such, the world has nevertheless been infected by a great cancer. Evil has invaded the world, and the chief cause is... the human being. The term the Bible most often uses to describe our own evil is *sin*. Simply speaking, sin is going against God's standards, either by transgression or omission. Sadly, one of the most dreadful consequences of this condition is that God cannot be seen and enjoyed as he once was by our

[4] *In Christ Alone*, ibid., 168.
[5] *The Lord's Prayer*, op. cit., 5ff.

first parents in the Garden. The good news of the gospel is that God devised a way for us to return to that unbroken fellowship. One day, we shall see him face to face. But for now things are dark and murky (1 Cor. 13:12). Our Father is in heaven, which means, at least in one sense, that he is not on earth.

So, where is heaven? Since the nineteenth century this term has become increasingly subjective, or just vague. Meant to give comfort, it lacks reality. And after the twentieth century, with its unprecedented destructiveness, heaven became nearly absent from most discourse. Biblically, heaven can mean the atmosphere around us. The rain and the snow come down from heaven (Isa. 55:9–11). Or it can mean the realm above the earth. The celestial heavens, sometimes translated the 'firmament,' refer to what we might call today 'outer space,' where the stars and the galaxies are (Gen. 1:14; Heb. 1:10).

Here, and in so much of the New Testament, heaven refers to the dwelling place of God. To use theological terms, God is transcendent and immanent. While we are told that 'the heavens, even the highest heaven, cannot contain God' (1 Kgs. 8:27), that God lives in a 'high and holy place' (Isa. 57:15), and that he is 'The Lord, the God of heaven' (2 Chron. 36:23; Dan. 2:37), yet also we are told that God is everywhere (he is immanent). While it is best not to try and think of heaven primarily in spatial terms, the image of the tabernacle, or the temple, or the sanctuary, that is, a dwelling place, is often used to describe where God lives (Heb. 8:2; Ex. 25:8). The most important consideration about heaven, in this sense, is the person who occupies it, and what effect the occupant has on us. Indeed, at times heaven is a synonym for God, as when people are described as 'looking up to heaven' (Matt. 14:19; Luke 9:16). Jesus himself came down from heaven, and returned to it (John 6:42; Acts 1:11). Heaven is the place where the angelic beings surround the throne of God (Ps. 148:2; Rev. 4:1–20; 11:19).

The *kingdom* of heaven, as we have seen, is the realm where God is present, where he rules, with all of his glory. It is the realm where all of the benefits we may receive from him are generated. This is the primary sense in which Our Lord used the term. Later in this prayer, he tells us to ask that God's will be done, 'on earth, as it is in heaven,' clearly implying that things here below are not as they should be, nor as they soon shall be (Matt. 6:10). Throughout the Gospels, Jesus refers to God either as his own heavenly Father, or as *our* heavenly Father, or *the* heavenly Father (Matt. 15:13; 18:35; Luke 11:13; etc.). In this Sermon, four times he calls God 'your *heavenly* Father,' or the equivalent (5:16, 45; 6:1; 7:11), once '*our* Father who is in heaven' (here, in the *Lord's Prayer*), and once 'my *heavenly* Father' (7:21). He identifies God in these same ways many times elsewhere. So the Father is in heaven.

Heaven is also the place to which the Lord brings believers. We are now in the heavenly places, and one day, at the resurrection, we shall be there fully and perfectly. We have here the famous 'already-not-yet' that characterizes so much in our Christian lives. In the letter to the Ephesians, Paul uses the expression 'the heavenlies' several times (1:3, 1:20; 2:6; 6:12). The heavenlies are where Christ went after his resurrection and ascension, where he now sits at God's right hand and rules over every power and name (Eph. 1:20–21). God has raised us up with Christ, and seated us with Christ in the heavenlies (2:6). This is to show us the extravagance of his gifts. Thus Paul says of us we already are in the heavenly places, receiving now the blessings of God through our union with Jesus Christ (1:3).

The heavenlies are also a work in progress. Not everything that will be settled in the new heavens and new earth is now already settled. Thus, again in Ephesians, we are told there are rulers and authorities in the heavenlies that need to hear about Christ's rule (3:10). The thought is astonishing: whenever the gospel is preached, not only earthly creatures like us hear and are affected, but heavenly ones as well. And significantly, we believers are doing battle not chiefly against visible forces, but against heavenly powers (6:12).[6] We must be careful neither to minimize this teaching, nor over-dramatize it. On the one hand, many Christians do not take the supernatural seriously, and do not calculate its reality into their worldview. They do this at their peril. Instead, they need to be apprised of the full force of darkness, as well as the full armor of God they have been given not only to resist but to overcome it. In the words of dual authors E. K. Simpson and F. F. Bruce, 'What fell embodiments of force and fraud, leagued against the Lord's Anointed, the noble army of Christian martyrs and confessors have been fortified to face!'[7] On the other hand, some think they see a devil behind every bush, and blame everything from being overweight to smoking on demons.[8] The Christian life is one of willpower, a mental, physical combat against temptations and sinful inclinations. To be sure this fight is conducted by faith, not relying on our merit, but on the strength Christ will give us. But we cannot lazily blame everything on demonic forces nor minimize our own responsibility.

The words heaven, heavenly places, kingdom of heaven, thus refer to a realm that is transcendent, above and beyond the earthly or visible world, but yet deeply affecting our world. The heavenly kingdom is the place from which God exercises his power. But it is also a place where spiritual beings are busy trying to destroy God's work. Only faith can fully recognize the reality of heaven in its various expressions. That is why Jesus says to Nicodemus, 'If I have told you earthly things and you do not believe, how can you believe if I tell you heavenly things?' (John 3:12). Here he was calling the new birth an 'earthly thing,' because the rabbi Nicodemus should have known about

---

[6] See the excellent article by Andrew T. Lincoln, ''The Heavenlies' in Ephesians, *New Testament Studies* 19/4, July, 1973, 468–483.

[7] E. K. Simpson & F. F. Bruce, *The Epistles to the Ephesians and Colossians*, Grand Rapids: Eerdmans, 1957, 144.

[8] I once heard an evangelist recount his casting out the 'demon of nicotine' from a victim.

it, based on his understanding of the Old Testament. Heavenly things would include the final appearance of the kingdom of God, the glorious rule of God and other such matters. But they would especially include what Jesus said next to Nicodemus: the Son of Man would descend from heaven, become accursed for the sake of his people, and then be able to ascend back to heaven, his people coming with him, having been saved from the curse they deserved (John 3:13–14).

In the end, believers will enjoy the new heavens and the new earth (Isa. 66:22). God is the creator of this final realm (Isa. 65:17). There will be the New Jerusalem, which has the tree of life available for the nations (Rev. 22:2). Again, the most important feature of the new heavens and the new earth is the presence of God, by whose light all the nations will walk (Rev. 21:22–24). God's servants will see his face there (Rev. 22:4).

It would therefore be a profound error to characterize heaven as a foggy, contentless or ideal reality in a Platonic way. Heavenly things are not less, but more contentful than earthly things.[9] If there is discontinuity between the things of earth and the things of heaven there is also continuity. Paul is anxious to shed his earthly body and enjoy the heavenly body that we shall one day put on (1 Cor. 15:40; 2 Cor. 5:2). There is a future heaven, into which we shall be safely placed at the right time (2 Tim. 4:18). But he also spoke of being in the heavenlies now, and experiencing its blessings, as well as the battles of heaven now. Similarly, the author of the Hebrews makes the contrast between heaven and earth, but he also alludes to our experiencing the full reality of heaven now (Heb. 9:23).

Hallowed be thy name

Identifying God as Father and situating him in heaven is the foundation for our worldview. Everything begins here. Behind the words is a host of theological and philosophical

---

[9] The logical argument, *a minori ad maius*.

notions. Simple on the surface, the truth of a heavenly Father is limitless in depth. We can, and we will, spend our lives, here and in eternity, going deeper and deeper into the fathomless wonder of ultimate reality.

Knowing this, and believing it, however, are not enough. For it is possible to understand and even accept this worldview without engaging it in a way that matters. Stating that God is a Father in heaven cannot just be an identification, something like an email address. No, we must enter the dance. The rest of the phrase, 'hallowed be thy name,' not only acknowledges the heavenly Father as the ultimate, the beginning, the meaning behind all things, but actually praises him for it. To put it simply, the *Lord's Prayer* is a prayer, and it begins as a prayer of worship. The prayer is not only that the name be holy for everyone, but to the one or ones praying, to you and me.

Adoring God is to express gratitude for what he has done, and for his generous nature. But adoration is more than gratitude. As C. S. Lewis put it in his thoughts about prayer, 'Gratitude exclaims, very properly, "How good of God to give me this." Adoration says, "What must be the quality of that Being whose far-off and momentary coruscations are like this!" One's mind runs back up the sunbeam to the sun.'[10]

The little pronoun *thy*, which we preserve from Elizabethan English in the Prayer is another reminder of the intimacy with which we may address the Father. In many languages there is a pointed difference between addressing a person as 'you' in the singular and 'you' in the plural. The French, for example, will address a new acquaintance as *vous* until asked to be more familiar, and use *tu* ('can we now *tutoi* each other?') The same for German with *sie* the formal and *du* the informal (we may begin to *dozen* instead of *siezen* one another). Until the Protestant Reformation, God was addressed in these

[10] C. S. Lewis, *Letters to Malcolm: Chiefly on Prayer*, New York: Harcourt, Brace & Jovanovich, 1963, 90.

languages with the formal pronoun. In modern English we can no longer emphasize this distinction, since both the second person singular and plural use *you*. Originally, in Elizabethan English, one could indeed stress intimacy with God by the use of *thee*; *thou* or *thine* meant the less formal singular than *you* (occasionally *ye*). Some conservative Quaker groups use *thee*, *thou* and *thine* to signify friendship with brothers and sisters.[11] Ironically some people still pray using these Elizabethan pronouns, but it is more a special prayer language for them than an expression of intimacy.[12] Most Protestants today, and an increasing number of Roman Catholics, address God as *you*, except when praying the *Lord's Prayer*!

Human beings are innately religious creatures. Not everyone likes to hear this, particularly people who prefer to remain skeptical and not engage in anything that resembles confession or liturgy and the like. When we think of religious people we tend to think of monks or church-goers and the like. But monasticism and church attendance are only outward expressions of heart commitments. If all we mean by religion is cultic or doctrinal elements, then being religious is not necessarily something desirable. Karl Barth (1886–1968) did not like the term religion, for it seemed to him to equal 'idolatry and self-righteousness, and in this way ... to be unbelief.'[13] His judgment is a bit harsh. Yet his motive was to safeguard the true, pure revelation from above, from earthly corruptions.

Religion is best understood not as ritual or idolatry, though it can be those, but as a heart-commitment, the worship of some first principle. While ideals or truths will be involved, religion,

[11] In Lancaster English the distinction is still made. A humorous exchange demonstrates the difference: to teach a child respect, the phrase is spoken, *Don't thee me, thee; I's you to thee!* ('Don't *thee* me, thee [i.e., 'you child']; I'm *you* to thee!').

[12] Even in the Revised Standard Version of the Bible (1952) the Elizabethan pronouns are used when addressing God in prayer.

[13] Karl Barth, *Church Dogmatics* 1.2.3 §17.

as the name suggests (*religare*, to bind together) is a worldview, held, sometimes consciously, sometimes not, by every human being, individually or collectively. Atheists qualify as religious because their heart commitment is to a worldview without God or gods. They may in some sense believe in humanity as the sole sufficient object of faith. Radical forms of atheism include Buddhism which believes in 'nothingness.' Zen Buddhism denies the existence of any god, yet believes in 'enlightenment.' So, no one is irreligious. As the famous Bob Dylan song puts it, 'You gotta serve somebody.' Biblically-oriented Christians serve the heavenly Father, and worship him as holy.

What are we praying when we say 'Hallowed be thy name'? The verb *be* here is in the subjunctive mood. We do not use it as much in English as we used to. Basically, the subjunctive signifies something that ought to be, rather than something that happens. Using the subjunctive, I might say, 'it was required that he *go* back to school.' Compare this to the indicative mood, 'he *went* back to school.' So the subjunctive can describe a state of affairs as well as the need to recognize it. Here, in the *Lord's Prayer*, we are saying, 'May your name be holy.' It already is, but may we recognize it, and praise you for it.

Holiness is a sadly outdated word today. We are rarely exhorted to call anything holy. Yet, the concept deserves to be anything but outmoded. The Greek word here in the Prayer is *hagiastheto*. The verb *hagiazo* means to declare holy, to consecrate. Here, in the aorist mood, it means, 'Holy be your name,' that is, 'your name has been, and is, and should evermore be holy.' The French translation has, 'que ton nom soit sanctifié,' or 'may your name be (made) holy.' Though God is intrinsically holy, we worshipers can still sanctify his name, by praising him and acknowledging his holiness. Throughout the Bible holiness means separation. That can be the separation of God as creator from the rest, a separation of being. Or it can mean separation from sinful or profane things. Certain people or even objects used in worship in Old Testament times were considered 'holy.'

Believers ought to grow in holiness (Eph. 1:4). The Christian community may be said to be holy (Col. 3:12). The church grows together into a holy temple (Eph. 2:21). Believers would greet one another with a 'holy kiss' (Rom. 16:16; 1 Cor. 16:20; 2 Cor. 13:12). Even the children born to a family with only one believer are considered holy (1 Cor. 7:14).

Most often, and most importantly, holiness is an attribute of God. Because God does not (and cannot) devote himself to a higher principle, his holiness affirms his self-sufficiency and autonomy. He is his own standard. He is holy, and therefore splendid, awe-inspiring. God is separate from his creatures in at least two ways. First, he is their Maker. He is the Creator, and we human beings are dependent creatures. A host of implications follow. He is eternal, we are time-bound. He is original, we are derivative. He is one God in three Persons, we are his image-bearers. He is the Father of lights in whom there is no variation or shadow due to change, whereas we are constantly changing (James 1:17). Second, there is another sense in which God is holy. He is utterly without moral stain. He is incapable of evil. He is pure and righteous. Jesus Christ is the perfect embodiment of holiness. Far more than the absence of sin, it is the full resolve to follow God's ways and perfectly (John 17:19). We, since the fall, are sadly tainted and corrupt. We are very far from the mark (Rom. 3:9–20). Of course, in the gospel, it is possible to grow in holiness (that is what the word *sanctification* actually means). We are even told to be holy, just as God is holy (Lev. 11:44; 1 Pet. 1:16; Heb. 12:10). But we will never attain the very same holiness as God, for that is an impossibility. God is by nature pure and holy. We can now only attain any kind of holiness by the grace of God.

So it is appropriate that identifying God as the Father in heaven, we should fall down and worship him. Worship need not be monotonous or colorless, any more than holiness is a cold, remote quality. Nor does worship have to be exclusively verbal, although words should always be near the center. The

Psalmist often declares that God is to be praised with music and singing. Because God is holy, exuberant praise is called for: 'I will sing praises to you with the lyre, O Holy One of Israel' (Ps. 71:22). Worship may, and must, be sober, yet always joyful in the most profound sense. Here is how John Calvin put it, 'Joy and thanksgiving expressed in prayer and praise according to the Word of God are the heart of the Church's worship.' Not that joy needs always to be exuberant. The Reformer, again, puts it this way: 'Joy is a quiet gladness of heart as one contemplates the goodness of God's saving grace in Christ Jesus.' The joy may not always be bubbly, but is always deeply real.

Our homeless mind

These opening words stand in stark contrast to much of our experience of the world. Jacques Attali, the French philosopher, has defined twenty-first-century people as 'nomads.' Humanity has always wandered, but now, with increasingly rapid means of communication and transportation, our planet is becoming a nomadic hyperempire, he says. He argues that we are moving to a chaotic global market with winners and losers.[14] Although he recognizes the dangers in such a world, Attali is hopeful that nomadism could lead to what he calls 'hyperdemocracy,' a sort of world order based on liberal economic values.

Similarly, as sociologist Peter Berger has described it, in a world that is secularized, the people are condemned to what he calls 'the homeless mind.'[15] Secularization continues to be a reality in Europe and in certain parts of North America. God is absent. What remains is an empty heaven. This means many people are homeless, not in the literal sense of having

---

[14] Jacques Attali, *A Brief History of the Future*, New York: Arcade/Skyhorse, 2009.

[15] Peter L. Berger, *The Homeless Mind*, New York: vintage, 1974. More recently Berger has nuanced his theory of secularization. The facts of widespread religious commitment lean against the simplistic approach that says mankind is becoming less religious. Still, much of the West is secular in all kinds of ways.

no shelter, but in the larger sense that they have no place to consider as a true place of rest, a spiritual abode.

While there is no doubt people are moving about the globe at a fantastic rate, there is not much cause to be hopeful. We desperately try to conquer space and time, the Internet being 'Exhibit A,' but this is not always a good thing. We are losing our sense of place, our sense of belonging to tradition. If Attali is right, which we hope he is not, we nomads are being governed by the most secular of hopes: humanism triggered by economic survival. Instead, the gospel teaches that 'man shall not live by bread alone.' To Attali's migrations toward hyperdemocracy, to Berger's homeless mind, the *Lord's Prayer* says, 'Our Father, who art in heaven, hallowed by thy name!' We will never reach human rights and liberty by wandering around the earth. We need a place to stand.

Whether nomads, or homeless secularists, we are, all of us, fatherless by nature. We have no home here. We are wanderers. The opening words of *Moby Dick* say it powerfully: 'Call me Ishmael.' The character Ishmael is an outcast. He has turned to the sea because he is alienated from society. In the last line of the novel, Ishmael refers to himself as an orphan. The book of Genesis makes this connection. Born to Abraham through Hagar, the servant woman, rather than his wife, Sarah, Ishmael is banished with his mother (Gen. 21:10). He is the lone truth-teller. When he says, 'I alone have escaped to tell thee,' his words reflect the messenger of doom in Job 1:15-19, who alone broke out to tell the patriarch the bad news of his children's demise.

But no! Instead, now we have a home. Our home is not here on earth, but we are like Abraham, who looked forward to the city that has foundations, whose designer and builder is God (Heb 11:10). We may be 'elect exiles of the dispersion' (1 Pet. 1:1), but yet we are 'a chosen race, a royal priesthood, a holy nation, a people for [God's] own possession,' and our purpose is to proclaim the excellencies of his name (1 Pet. 2:9). 'For my father and my mother have forsaken me, but the Lord will take me in' (Ps. 27:10). We are ambassadors for Christ sent to implore our listeners to be reconciled to God (2 Cor. 5:20). We do not go as aimless nomads or hapless orphans but as members of the family of God, children of the Father, sent to tell others of the good news of adoption (John 16:25; Gal. 4:5; Eph. 1:5). Our Father, who art in heaven. Hallowed be thy name!

Hymn

The God of Abraham praise, who reigns enthroned above;
Ancient of everlasting days, and God of love;
Jehovah, great I AM, by earth and heaven confessed:
I bow and bless the sacred Name for ever blessed.

The God of Abraham praise, at whose supreme command
from earth we rise, and seek the joys at his right hand;
we all on earth forsake, its wisdom, fame and power;
and him our only portion make, our Shield and Tower.

The goodly land we see, with peace and plenty blessed:
a land of sacred liberty and endless rest;
there milk and honey flow, and oil and wine abound,
and trees of life for ever grow, with mercy crowned.

There dwells the Lord, our King, the Lord, our Righteousness,
triumphant o'er the world and sin, the Prince of Peace;
on Zion's sacred height his kingdom he maintains,
and, glorious with his saints in light, for ever reigns.

The God who reigns on high, the great archangels sing,
and 'Holy, holy, holy,' cry, 'Almighty King!'
Who was and is the same, and evermore shall be:
Jehovah, Father, great I AM, we worship thee.'

The whole triumphant host give thanks to God on high;
'Hail, Father, Son, and Holy Ghost' they ever cry;
hail, Abraham's God and mine; I join the heavenly lays;
all might and majesty are thine, and endless praise!

(Thomas Olivers, 1770, paraphrase of Daniel
ben Judah's *Sabbath Eve Prayer*, 14th century)

5

Thy Kingdom Come, Thy Will Be Done, on Earth as It Is in Heaven

In chapter 4 (of Revelation) God's sovereignty is seen as it is already fully acknowledged in heaven. This establishes it as the true reality which must in the end also prevail on earth. On earth the powers of evil challenge God's role and even masquerade as the ultimate power over all things, claiming divinity. But heaven is the sphere of ultimate reality: what is true in heaven must become true on earth. (Richard Bauckham)

The already-not-yet

We have previously discovered how the kingdom is a central theme in the *Lord's Prayer*. Everything in the prayer relates to the coming of God's kingdom. Now, in this petition we straightforwardly ask the Lord for his kingdom to come. And we do so by pairing it up with the request, 'thy will be done,' and then adding, 'on earth as it is in heaven.'

What is the shape of this coming kingdom? What exactly should we be praying for, and what will the answers look like? In our earlier discussion of the kingdom we mentioned the calling of mankind to glorify God and enjoy him forever. The particulars of this high calling are contained in the so-called 'cultural mandate.' Because of the mercy of God, this calling was not abrogated at the fall, but rather given new meaning and depth in the era of redemption. Throughout the Old Testament, the cultural mandate (Gen. 1:26ff.) is reiterated in various ways. Psalm 8 invites us to contemplate the significance of the human being within the vast realm of the universe. To the question, 'What is man that you are mindful of him,' comes the answer, 'Yet you have made him a little lower than the heavenly beings and crowned him with glory and honor. You have given him dominion over the works of your hands...' (vv.4, 5-6). To the exiles in Babylon, Jeremiah writes, counter-intuitively, that the Israelites should build houses, plant gardens, marry and have children, and work for the welfare of the city (Jer. 29:4ff.).

This cultural mandate intensifies in the New Testament. Jesus is identified with the man of Psalm 8 in subjection to whom God has put everything (Heb. 2:6-8). At present we do not yet see everything in subjection to him, but we have our marching orders: 'Go therefore and make disciples of all the nations...' (Heb. 2:9; Matt. 28:19). Subjection of all things to Christ, and making disciples of all the nations, these are expressions of the cultural mandate, now given its highest expression as the power of God to salvation (Rom. 1:17). The kingdom of God wherein this subjection and reordering occur has come, and is coming in the world today, and will arrive in all its finality in the world to come.

Richard Bauckham has studied the Book of Revelation for much of his career. In his excellent book, *The Theology of the Book of Revelation*, he sees a strong connection between the *Lord's Prayer* and the apocalypse: 'The whole of revelation could be regarded as a vision of the fulfillment of the first three petitions of the Lord's Prayer: 'Your name be hallowed, your kingdom come, your will be done, on earth as it is in heaven' (Matt. 6:9–10).' He goes on to say that in the Rome of the author John's day, God's name was not hallowed, nor his will done; instead evil ruled through oppression and exploitation. 'But in chapter 4, he sees in heaven, the sphere of ultimate reality, the absolute holiness, righteousness and sovereignty of God. From this vision of God's name hallowed and God's will done in heaven, it follows that his kingdom must come to earth.'[1]

To put it in a well-known phrase, we are now in the already-not-yet of the coming of the kingdom. Within this perspective things can become distorted. Many of the Jews in the first century were convinced that God's kingdom would indeed come soon, through a military coup. When Jesus came he disappointed those who were looking for a leader to overthrow the Roman oppressors. He taught things such as, 'My kingdom is not of this world' (John 18:36), and rebuked his disciples when they wanted to fight (Luke 22:49–51). The great day of God's judgment would come, but not right away. As the Apostles' Creed has it, 'he will come again to judge both the quick and the dead.' The judgment will occur on a day and hour of his determination, one that will not be revealed to us until it happens (Matt. 24:36). That this day will come is not in question. It will come as a surprise to many: 'But the day of the Lord will come like a thief, and then the heavens will pass away with a roar...' (2 Pet. 3:10; cf. 1 Thess. 5:2). Because of this we should not be tempted to say, as do certain cults, that the day of the Lord has already come (2 Thess. 2:2). It will be a great and magnificent day (Acts 2:20). It will be a day when believers in Christ will be publically acquitted (1 Cor. 1:8). It will be a day of judgment for those who refuse to follow Christ (Rev. 20:11–15).

---

[1] Richard Bauckham, *The Theology of the Book of Revelation*, Cambridge: Cambridge University Press, 1993, 40.

Judgment and renewal

In the meantime, as we wait for that day, there is plenty of divine activity. The 'already' of the already-not-yet is real enough. First, when the kingdom comes there are judgments. Not the final judgment, but nevertheless true judgments. Upheavals, wars, disasters of all kinds, these are regarded in the Bible not as 'accidents' but as days of reckoning. Jesus predicted that before the end there would be all kinds of tribulations (Luke 24:6ff.). The Book of the Revelation tells us that judgments occur as a series of seven seals being opened, or a series of trumpets being blown (Rev. 6; 8:6ff.). We must be cautious to avoid simple equations in our visible world between particular evils and particular tribulations. We can rarely know for sure what the connections are. Still, the kingdom comes with judgments.

Second, though, the kingdom comes with renewal. Throughout Isaiah the *Servant of the Lord* is described as the one who would enable not only the Jews to return to their country, but Jews and Gentiles alike to return to the Lord who saves them.

> He says:
> It is too light a thing that you should be my servant
>   to raise up the tribes of Jacob
> And to bring back the preserved of Israel;
>   I will make you as a light for the nations,
>   That my salvation may reach to the end of the earth.
>
> (Isa. 48:6)

We should pause to consider what is often the case with Old Testament prophecies. They rather stagger the imagination. Isaiah wrote during Israel's decline (c. 740–700 BC). Rife with corruption, the Lord compared this people to Sodom and Gomorrah (1:10). Their worship was hypocritical (1:11; 66:3). They failed to defend the fatherless and the widow (1:17; 9:17; 10:2). And indeed the judgment came and the people were defeated and sent into exile. It looked as though the days of Israel were done. A blip on the historical screen. Their power was no greater than that of the Russians in Diaspora after the Revolution.

Instead of offering a few timid prophecies stating that things might get better, or that God would do something modest, Isaiah tells the people that the Servant of the Lord would not only restore their fortunes, raising up the tribes of Jacob and bringing them back to the land, but that the Gentiles would find salvation through him, and that salvation would reach to the ends of the earth. After that God would establish a new heaven and a new earth where nothing of the present world order would be remembered (65:17). These promises are extravagant, unreasonable, impossible... and yet, quite true. Though the Servant must suffer horribly, yet, by his stripes we are healed, and the Lord has laid on the servant, his Son, the iniquities of us all (53:5-6). Because of this substitutionary atonement God's people, Jew and Gentile alike, will come back to him like the bride temporarily deserted but then fully restored because of God's everlasting love of compassion (54:8).

We who live on this side of the cross of Christ have the advantage of knowing the way everything turned out. The risen Christ commissioned his church to go and make disciples of the *ethne*, the nations, assuring the church of his powerful, effectual presence until the end of the ages (Matt. 28:19-20). That same authority came down to the disciples at Pentecost, when the Holy Spirit filled them and gave them tongues of fire. What was lost at the Tower of Babel is now being restored through the uniting work of the Spirit (Acts 2:1-4). This was at last the Father's promised Holy Spirit to Jesus the Son, who promptly and generously poured out the gift on his people (Acts 2:33). Great numbers began to be added to the church (Acts 2:41, 47; 5:14; 11:24). So the Jews became a light to the Gentiles, and when the gospel was preached to the Gentiles they rejoiced and gloried in God's word, and many were saved

(Acts 13:48).[2] Even when the Jews refused to believe, that became an opportunity for the Gentiles to enter in. Yet God would not forget his ancient people, and, so, by the Gentiles believing, they would be provoked, as if by jealousy, and come back themselves (Rom. 11:11, 14). Thus all people, Jew and Gentile alike become candidates for salvation, on condition they receive the gospel by faith and repentance.

Paul and the other apostles took the gospel to the entire world as it was then known, using the highways of the Roman Empire. Even Ethiopia would hear the gospel through Philip's exposition of a portion of Isaiah to a certain God-fearing eunuch (Acts 8:26–40). How far, then, would the gospel of the kingdom extend? Here we are some twenty one centuries later and we may truly say that there is no continent, and very few countries, if any, where the gospel has not been preached and received. Estimates are difficult to make, but at least in name, there are well over two billion Christians on the planet, easily the largest of the world's religions. The next largest, Islam, counts about one and a half billion, however the Muslim population is heavily concentrated in North Africa, the Middle East, and a few countries in Asia. Perhaps the numbers do not tell us as much as the eloquent testimonies of the different ways the Christian faith manifests itself in the different locations.

How far and how long?

If there is an 'already,' there is also a 'not-yet.' In one important sense, the kingdom is yet to come, just as God's will is yet to be done. When asked about the end times, Jesus told his disciples that 'this gospel of the kingdom will be proclaimed throughout the whole world as a testimony to all nations, and then the end will come' (Matt. 24:14, see 26:13; Mark 14:9; Rom. 10:18; Rev. 16:14). Thus, among other features characterizing these

---

[2] Paul actually quotes Isaiah 49:6 in his speech to the Jews at Antioch as proof that things were going according to plan (Acts 13:47).

end times are world missions. Not only in the proclamation of the gospel, leading to conversion, but the disciple-making mandated by the Lord just before his ascension (Matt. 28:19). The apostles were certainly aware of this new world order coming into existence as the result of their preaching (Col. 1:6, 23).

How much farther will the gospel of the kingdom extend until the end of history? We simply do not know. There have been a good many false guesses about the end of the world. Some of the most notable include Martin Luther, who said that the end was 'just around the corner.' Many more precise predictions were made in more recent times. For example, the leader of the Adventists, William Miller, predicted Christ's second coming to be before March 21, 1844. When it did not happen, he adjusted to April 18, 1844. When that date passed another Millerite, Samuel S. Snow, predicted the date to be October 22, 1844. When none of these worked out, people deemed it 'the Millerite Great Disappointment.' Similar predictions, adjustments, and disappointments are found among the Jehovah's Witnesses. The first president of the Watch Tower Society, Charles Taze Russell, taught that Christ would come again, but invisibly: in 1874, followed by the resurrection of the saints in 1875, and their rapture in 1878. The final judgment, he proclaimed, would come in 1914. When these events did not occur, several readjustments were made, and finally the Watch Tower Society admitted to building up false hope, based on erroneous calculations.

Although Jesus specifically warned not to speculate about times and dates (Matt. 24:36; Acts 1:7), yet that was not meant to lead us into complacency. Quite the opposite. We do know that the Second Coming will be a surprise. Jesus will come like a thief in the night (Matt. 24:43; 1 Thess. 5:2). We also know that certain signs of the end will occur, or, are occurring. Negative ones include false prophets, heresies, wars, persecutions, antichrists. But more positively, as we just mentioned, world mission will occur and succeed. Perhaps the apostles themselves could not have imagined the extensiveness of world missions, if only because they lacked knowledge of the vastness of the planet and its populations. However, they certainly knew that the gospel would be extensively preached. When Luke records that Paul went throughout the Roman Empire, ending up in Rome itself, he showed awareness that the kingdom had come to the very center of the then-known world.

Idols for destruction

Along with the positive fruits of the kingdom's presence, there must be the destruction of all that opposes it. When Jesus preached the kingdom it was often in contrast to the evils of the present life. Kingdom preaching was accompanied by healing people's diseases (Matt. 4:23; 9:35). The poor in spirit and those who are persecuted for righteousness' sake will be given the kingdom (Matt. 5:3, 10). Jesus explains that the kingdom comes with violence (Matt. 11:12; Luke 16:16). Most likely this means that those who are entering the kingdom must do so with 'violent' zeal, not literally, but in terms of their passion and eagerness. By implication, there must be a struggle against all the forces that would keep us from such an entry. Paul often uses language of violence or struggle to describe the Christian life. In Ephesians 6 he urges us to 'take up the whole armor of God,' being fully equipped to withstand the evil day and remain firm (Eph. 6:13ff.).

According to the biblical worldview, one of the chief obstacles to the worship of God is idolatry. Idols in ancient times were often objects of stone or wood which were believed to be the dwelling place of a divinity or supernatural power. The countries that surrounded ancient Israel were generally polytheistic. The pantheon believed by the Mesopotamians comprised some 1,500 gods, including Ishtar, Marduk and Sin (the moon-god). The gods of fertility were especially worshiped. Likewise, the Canaanites worshiped fertility gods such as El, Baal and Astarte. Worshiping these gods was considered an abomination to the Israelites. According to the ten commandments, the first is to have no other gods beside the Lord, and the second banned all images for use in worship. This was a radical innovation in the Ancient Near East. Idols were 'a terror' (Jer. 50:38); they were 'trouble and sorrow' (Isa. 66:3); they were shapeless and speechless (Ez. 20:31). Indeed, one of the central critiques of idolatry in the Old Testament was its inability to interact personally with human beings. Habbakuk gives a typical apologetic against idolatry:

> What profit is an idol
> when its maker has shaped it,
> a metal image, a teacher of lies?
> For its maker trusts in his own creation
> when he makes speechless idols (Hab. 3:18).

Notice the irony here: a maker trusts his creation. Paul similarly denounces the worship of the creature instead of the Creator, who is clearly known (Rom. 1:20–23).

Why do people engage in such irrational practices? Because it is the only alternative to the worship of the true God. Everyone is religious, as we have mentioned above. Everyone worships something or someone. If not God, then the only other place to turn is the creation. Of course, the creation may be objects and statues, but it may also be ideologies or ideals, such as beauty, or love, or power. For Karl Marx (1818–1883) the object of 'worship' was dialectical materialism, the idea that the material (nothing spiritual) comes before anything like human consciousness or values, and that history moves through a series of conflicts emerging from the material world.[3] For Henri Bergson (1859–1941) it was duration, intuition, and the 'élan vital,' a sort of life-force which explains evolution in a non-

---

[3] Actually, Marx never used the exact expression 'dialectical materialism,' which is likely from his disciple Joseph Dietzgen. However, the expression suits Marx well.

mechanistic manner. For some first-century Jews, then, a political overthrow of the Romans was an idolatrous view of the end times. Idols can also be psychologically driven. Addictions or obsessions are types of idols. Gambling, sex, prosperity can be idols. But so can conditions such as false guilt, envy, self-pity, pride, co-dependency, even anger. The apostle Paul denounces covetousness as a form of idolatry (Col. 3:5).

Dick Keyes has given us a fascinating account of how idolatry works.[4] He suggests that because idolatry is a counterfeit for two fundamental human callings, idols often come in pairs. God is immanent. Therefore one kind of idolatry is creating a 'nearby god.' God is also transcendent, so the other kind of idol is a 'faraway god.' The nearby idol results from our need for dominion, at first a proper need, instituted by God at the creation, but now gone wrong because of our desire to tyrannize. The faraway idol comes from our need to trust. Again, trust is a good thing, but in the fallen world it goes wrong. Abundant examples of these paired idols can be found in the Scriptures. Jeremiah scorns idols which resemble scarecrows in a melon patch (Jer. 10:5). This idol is practical and functional, it gives one control. The faraway idol is represented by Isaiah's critique of forsaking the Lord and substituting a 'table for Fortune and... mixed cups of mixed wine for Destiny' (Isa. 65:11). These are mysterious forces that cannot really be controlled. Contemporary examples also abound. Consider the realm of money. For example, those who trust in their nest-egg or savings account to provide a better standard of living are worshiping nearby idols. At the same time the very same people might put their trust in some hope that prosperity can make one secure, young, powerful, etc. Perhaps the faraway god is simply the trust in hard work as deserving of prosperity.[5]

---

[4] Dick Keyes, 'The Idol Factory,' in *No God but God*, Chicago: Moody Press, 1992, 29–48.

[5] Ibid., 41.

Idolatry is degrading. It not only demeans God, but also the idolater. We become like the idols we worship. Psalm 115:4–8 explains that though idols are deaf and dumb, those who make them become like them.[6] One horrible example of this is the move from the so-called 'sexual revolution' to the ideal of 'safe sex.' Roughly speaking, from the late 1950s, aided and abetted by the Playboy culture, we were told that we should drop our prudish ways and engage in sex when and where we would like to. If anything untoward happened, not to worry, we have technology to save us. So, for example, if free sex resulted in an unwanted pregnancy, we can have a therapeutic abortion. But then, beginning in the 1980s, we began to learn about HIV-AIDS. In layperson's terms, this virus attacks the immune system, until finally the body is unable to protect itself from various infections and tumors. Death is the inevitable result. The virus is protracted by unprotected sex. At least that is where it all began. Sadly, it can be caught with unclean needles, contact with saliva, or even or in the womb. There is a simple remedy for HIV-AIDS: practice fidelity. If people had sexual relations only within the bonds of marriage, in a few decades the disease would go away. What have we chosen instead? To keep the idol of free sex. Now what we are told is that we need to be a great deal more careful, use birth-control, etc. In a word, we now must practice 'safe sex,' which is a drastically impoverished version of sexuality, devoid of the romantic excitement of a revolution. To put it one way, you can now have sex without killing each other, if you are very, very cautious. Rather than give up the idol, we become diminished, dependent, and fairly foolish.

Toward the abundant life

When the kingdom of God breaks-in, idols are shattered. We now have the power to flee from idolatry (1 Cor. 10:14). But

---

[6] See G. K. Beale, *We Become What We Worship: A Biblical Theology of Idolatry*, Downers Grove: InterVarsity Press, 2008.

then, it is not enough to leave idolatry behind, for we need to build our new lives on the basis of the worship of God. We wish to become joyful, free and obedient servants of the king, citizens of his kingdom. All that was lost, all that is corrupted, is being rebuilt, raised from the dead. 'Behold, I am making all things new,' the one seated on the throne tells us (Rev. 21:5). Not, 'I *will* make all things new,' which of course he will in the new heavens and new earth, but 'I *am making*,' which is in the present tense. If our vision for the coming of the kingdom is anything less than all-encompassing, then we have not fully grasped the radical breach with falsity and idols provided in the gospel. The gospel, as Paul puts it, is the 'power of God for salvation' (Rom. 1:17). Salvation is nothing but comprehensive renewal.

Where do we see this power at work? Of course, a primary place is missions. From the earliest days of the church, the good news has been spread far and wide. Missions! With over two millennia of hindsight we can see the many ways in which missions has gone into every land and every people group. One trend that has recently come to our attention is the astonishing growth of the church in the global south. At the turn of the twentieth century there were about nine million Christians in all of Africa. By 2000 that number had risen to 380 million. Today it is well over 500 million. This story, with variants, can be reproduced in many parts of the global south, including Latin America, many parts of South Asia, but also in more northern countries such as South Korea, parts of Russia and its bordering countries, and in many parts of China.[7] Again, while the numbers are impressive, they do not tell the important part of the story.

The recent shifts in global mission from the North to the global South have often been noted. Besides the astonishing numerical growth of the church in places such as Latin

---

[7] Estimates are difficult to make, but there may be as many as 100 million Christians in China.

America, Africa and South Asia, there is also their remarkable vitality. At the 1998 decennial Lambeth Conference in Great Britain, a ten-year gathering of all leaders from the worldwide Anglican Church to assess the present and look into the future, a surprising note was sounded. The church was told it needed to do better in evangelism, the care of the poor, spiritual renewal, and gospel witness in pluralistic societies. The surprise was not the reiteration of the timeless message embodied in these themes, but the source: it was voiced mostly from African Anglican church leaders. Also, slowly but surely, churches in the global south are beginning to 'own' the gospel and not simply mimic the way Westerners think about it.[8] This means various things. For one, as Philip Jenkins argues, believers from the global south tend to read the Bible more literally than northerners.[9] They also tend to do theology with a greater emphasis on missions than Europeans. And they are extremely aware of the needs of the poor.

The kingdom has not fully come in the global South, however, so our prayer is still pertinent. One of the features of such rapid growth is how wide it is, but how thin as well. There is a desperate need for leadership training and theological education in many places. Without it, the danger is great of a return to pagan religion, or to false messages such as the health and wealth gospel. Furthermore, in many places where

[8] Many studies are being produced, tracking these trends in global Christianity. See, Lammin Sanneh & Joel A. Carpenter, *The Changing Face of Christianity: Africa, the West, and the World*, New York: Oxford University Press, 2005; Philip Jenkins, *The New Faces of Christianity: Believing the Bible in the Global South*, New York: Oxford University Press, 2006; Miriam Adenay, *Kingdom without Borders: The Untold Story of Global Christianity*, Downers Grove: InterVarsity Press, 2009; *Global Missiology for the Twenty First Century: The Igassu Dialogue*, William B. Taylor, ed., Grand Rapids: Baker Academic, 2001.

[9] *The New Faces of Christianity*, op. cit., 18 ff. At the same Lambeth Conference of 1998 a motion from North America to make homosexuality compatible with Christian values was rejected 526-70, the majority being mostly from the global South based on their unembroidered reading of the Bible.

the churches are growing, so also is persecution. So, a great deal of work needs to be done in these growing churches to guide them into more depth. There is a crying need for basic discipleship. Training is greatly needed not only in biblical studies but in other disciplines, such as ethics in the broadest sense: the application of the gospel to every area of life, business, politics, health care and family. Outsiders are often astonished to learn that the conflict between the Hutu and the Tutsi tribe that led to the slaughter of over one million people was a sort of class warfare, wherein both sides were Christians. What kind of Christian faith is unable to ignore the plain teaching of James 1:9-10, which urges the lowly to know his exalted status in Christ, and the rich to cultivate proper humility? The answer, presumably, is, a very superficial one. Westerners are in no position to cast the first stone, with our phony bank loans, our internet pornography, our corrupt city politics, etc., despite the large number of churches on so many street corners. It is just to say that, however exciting the growth of the church in the global south is to behold, we do not have a panacea there.

Stories about how the gospel reaches people can be riveting. When I was a new Christian I was given several books by Isobel Kuhn. The story of her own conversion is deeply moving. Isobel Selina Miller (1901-1957) was born in Canada to a believing family. At university she more or less threw away her Christian beliefs. Then the discovery that her fiancé was unfaithful sent her into a deep blue funk. Just as she was about to take her own life she remembered her father, a Presbyterian lay preacher, telling her of the wonders of the gospel. She had feared that believing might be only a mental opiate. But she remembered a line from Dante, 'In his will is our peace.'[10] She knew she needed that peace, and asked God to give it to her, vowing that if he did, she would serve him wherever he sent her. The peace

---

[10] Dante Alighieri, *Paradisio*, Canto III.

came. She went to Bible school. Isobel (known as 'Belle') was eventually called to reach the Lisu people. She joined the China Inland Mission. With her husband, John Becker Kuhn, they worked with the Lisu people on the China-Myanmar border. Evangelism had been going on with the Lisu at least since the pioneering work of James O. Fraser (1886-1938) who became a mentor and friend of the Kuhns. Fraser learned the language, then produced a written version of it. After the communists forced the Kuhns out, they continued to work with the Lisu of Thailand. Previous to becoming believers the Lisu were a brutal people, and ruled by Opium warlords. Constantly plagued by illness, challenging living conditions, and, often quite literally, demonic oppression, the Kuhns soldiered on, and saw remarkable changes take place. Belle was quite creative. For example, she built a 'Rainy Season Bible School.' Since no one could do much during the heavy rains, why not study the Scriptures? Today, nearly sixty years after her death, some 300,000 Lisu people are Christians, meeting in over 1,300 locations. Over 75,000 Bibles have been printed in their language. The churches are alive and well, though in need of more trained pastors. Isobel Kuhn's legacy is palpable.

Any time a sinner comes to faith, there is high drama. But most of the time, while the angels in heaven rejoice at the rescue of a lost soul, the change may be anonymous here on earth. When a child, brought up in a Christian home, matures into an adult faith, a miracle has occurred. The drama is no less significant than when a high-profile person turns around in the limelight. All of us, whether noticed or not, come to the gospel from a deeply sinful condition, which the Apostle Paul bleakly describes as 'following the course of this world, following the prince of the power of the air,' and being 'by nature children of wrath' (Eph. 2:2-3). When we enter into saving faith among other things we change our allegiance. We are, as it were, wrenched out of a life of loyalty to the world with all of its corruption, and set free to live a new life in Christ. We have been raised with Christ and now our life is hidden with Christ in God (Col. 3:1–3). When the kingdom is fully come we will appear with Christ in glory (v. 4).

When the kingdom comes, to use an expression from Francis Schaeffer, there is substantial healing. That healing takes place in several areas of life. We may be healing from a distorted relation to money and possessions. We may be healing from tensions in personal relationships. Wherever the fall has affected us, there can be substantial healing. Schaeffer qualified this by reminding us that there would not be perfection in the present life. He used to say, 'If you want perfection or nothing, you will get nothing every time.' Yet the healing is real nevertheless.

Wherever we are, whatever our issues, we are in the depths. Not only unbelievers, but believers can exclaim, 'Out of the depths, I cry to you, O Lord!'

> Out of the depths I cry to you, O Lord!
>> O Lord, hear my voice!
> Let your ears be attentive to the voice of my pleas for mercy!
> If you, O Lord, should mark iniquities,
>> O Lord, who could stand?
> But with you there is forgiveness
>> That you may be feared.
> I wait for the Lord, my soul waits,
>> And in his word I hope
> My soul waits for the Lord,
>>> more than watchmen for the morning,
>>> more than watchmen for the morning.
> O Israel, hope in the Lord!
>> For with the Lord there is steadfast love,
>> And with him is plentiful redemption.
>> And he will redeem Israel from all his iniquities (Ps. 130).

Psalm 130 is one of the most often set to music throughout the history of the church. And for good reason. One classic melody was composed by Martin Luther, and inspired by Gregorian chant. It begins with a descending fifth, signifying the depth of the distraught soul waiting for the Lord. Luther had it sung at his own funeral. It appears in the Huguenot Psalter, and was often set to four-part harmony in the later French Reformed music world. J. S. Bach composed one of his most beautiful chorale preludes for organ based on the tune. In modern times, in the more classical vein, Arvo Pärt set the Psalm using his haunting, minimalist chanting, building more and more, until the listener indeed reaches the surface, out of the depths, into the hope of plentiful redemption. The popular singing group, Sovereign Grace, has a folk version of the Psalm, using as a refrain, 'More than watch men for the morning, I will wait for you, my God.'

When God's kingdom comes, it opens the gates of heaven to those who are in the depths, whether because of their sin, or because of oppression, or both. Those who belong to God's kingdom belong as a people of hope. While there is forgiveness and relief now, we wait, we wait like watchmen for the full redemption he will bring in his own good time.

What should Christians be looking for when they pray, 'thy kingdom come'? Christian hope is realistic. No utopian vision, it knows to wait rather than precipitate. Not a passive wait, but one that develops patience.

One of the areas of life most difficult to have clarity about is human sexuality. There is a great deal of gender and identity confusion, particularly in the West. Gay marriage, or, as the French put it, 'marriage for all,' is on the rise and shows no sign of being halted. The Bible is clear on the nature of marriage: it should be monogamous and heterosexual. Does that mean the homosexuals are evil, or far more sinful than straight people? The remarkable testimony of Rosaria Champagne Butterfield gives great insights into this question.[11] She was a practicing lesbian and an activist leader in the gay community at

---

[11] Rosaria Champagne Butterfield, *The Secret Thoughts of an Unlikely Convert*, Pittsburgh: Crown & Covenant, 2012.

the college where she taught. Through the beautiful, patient testimony of a loving Christian community, led by its pastor, she became a follower of Christ. At first she was not altogether sure why homosexuality was wrong. Things came together for her when she looked into the story of Sodom and Gomorrah. As many had, Rosaria assumed that the predominant sin in Sodom was homosexuality. As she looked deeper into the story, and into the rest of the Bible, she began to conclude that homosexuality was but one manifestation of a far deeper problem, the problem of pride. When she read Ezekiel's account of Sodom, she was surprised to discover that the prophet's list of accusations included pride, affluence, lack of mercy which amounted to haughtiness and led to abominations.[12]

When we pray, 'thy kingdom come,' what are we asking for? Basically, we are asking that this world and its people be so submitted to the Lord God that their worship and their lives, their entire lives, may be ordered by the gospel. As we have seen, this has already begun to happen, and will continue to occur until Christ returns to earth to deliver its final installment. Those captured by the King and placed into his kingdom, will be able to say, 'hallowed be thy name.' Joachim Jeremias puts it eloquently:

> Every accession to power by an earthly ruler is accompanied by homage in words and gestures. So it will be when God enters upon his rule. Then men will do homage to him, hallowing his name: 'Holy, holy, holy, is the Lord God Almighty, who was and is and is to come' (Rev. 4:8).[13]

Doing homage means far more than verbal praise. It means orienting all of life around God's kingdom purposes and his holy will.

---

[12] Ibid, 30. The passage is Ezekiel 16:48–50.
[13] *The Lord's Prayer*, op. cit., 21–22.

Thy will be done

Often in Hebrew literature two phrases are put into parallel, the second confirming, or complementing the first. For example, 'Your word is a lamp to my feet and a light for my path,' (Ps. 119:105). This is known as *synonymous* parallelism, because the second phrase restates the same thought, though in a slightly extended manner. Another type of parallelism is *antithetical* parallelism, saying the same thing from the opposite end. 'The integrity of the upright guides them, but the crookedness of the treacherous destroys them' (Prov. 11:3) is such an example. Then there is *synthetical* parallelism, in which a second thought complements, or completes the first. The first verse of Psalm 42 has such a construction: 'As a deer pants for flowing streams, so pants my soul for you, O God.'[14]

While *The Lord's Prayer* is not narrowly a poem, some of it does follow the patterns of Hebrew poetry. Thus, 'Thy kingdom come, thy will be done,' is an example of synthetic parallelism. The coming of the kingdom, as we have seen, is a central consideration in all of the New Testament. It means the coming of the great king to establish his rule and his righteousness. Doing God's will is certainly an extension of this establishment. However, it represents a more detailed application of this rule and righteousness. It represents conformity to God's purposes.

God's will is one of his attributes. Here is what the great Reformed Theologian, Hermann Bavinck says:

> Everything derives from God's will: creation and preservation (Rev. 4:11), government (Prov. 21:1; Dan. 4:35; Eph. 1:11), Christ's suffering (Luke 22:42), election and reprobation (Rom. 9:15ff.), regeneration (James 1:18), sanctification (Phil. 2:13), the suffering of believers (1 Pet. 3:17), our life

---

[14] I am well aware of the difficulty of limiting parallelism to just these three types. For a richer presentation of various kinds of Hebrew parallels, see James L. Kugel, *The Idea of Biblical Poetry: Parallelism and Its History*. New Haven, Connecticut: Yale University Press, 1981, esp. 68ff.

and lot (James 4:15; Acts 18:21; Rom. 15:32), even the most
minute details of life (Matt. 10:29, etc.).[15]

This sounds absolutist, and could easily be mistaken for
determinism. Indeed, some religions, such as Islam, do have
a fatalist god. But not in the Christian faith. Bavinck goes on
to explain that there is considerable variation within the will
of God. 'But though he wills all creatures as means and for his
own sake, he wills some more than others to the degree they
are more direct and suitable means for his glorification... For
the free will of God is as richly variegated as the whole world
is.'[16] Three examples can illustrate this variegation. First, while
God loves all of creation, he especially loves his people. And
while he loves his people, he loves his only begotten Son even
more. Second, while evil is somehow decreed by God's will, in
no way is evil the same kind of object of his will as the good.
As we have already seen, The *Westminster Confession* states that
while God ordains everything that comes to pass, yet he is not
the author of sin (WCF III.1). And third, we may distinguish
between what God decrees (his decretive will) and what he
prescribes (his prescriptive will). Throughout biblical history
we see a difference between what God will make happen and
what he wants to happen. He wants Abraham to sacrifice Isaac,
but does not let it happen (Gen. 22). He wants Pharaoh to let
the people of Israel go, but then hardens his heart so that it
cannot happen (Ex. 4:21). He commands us not to condemn
the innocent, yet allows just that to happen to his Son at the
cross (Acts 2:23). He does not desire the death of a sinner, yet
he in fact does not have mercy upon all (1 Tim. 2:4).

Another way of expressing this same truth is in the language
of covenant. God indeed is the one who ordains all things. But

---

[15] Herman Bavinck, *Reformed Dogmatics*, vol. 2, 'God and Creation,' John Bolt,
  ed., John Vriend, transl., Grand Rapids: Baker Academic, 2004, 229.
[16] Ibid., 241.

he has made his creation with real significance, where choice is valid and consequences are real. How can he do this? By entering (with divine condescension, as the older theologies would put it) into covenant relation with his creatures. As we discussed earlier, in the section, 'Why Pray?' God's sovereignty does not abolish the need for prayer, but rather sustains it. That means that in one sense, by prayer and repentance we can change God's mind. Several passages in Scripture tell us as much. A dramatic case is that of Jonah's successful mission to the corrupt Ninevites. When they heard him, they repented of their evils, and God relented from the judgment he had threatened to bring (Jon. 3:9-10). Indeed, it is a principle that if a corrupt nation turns from its evil, God will relent and have mercy (Jer. 18:8). The word in Hebrew is a strong term, meaning to repent, to rue his intentions.

So, while ultimately God decrees all things immovably, yet in relation to his people, he can indeed be moved: he answers prayer and changes his mind. If you think about it, unless this be true, the entire *Lord's Prayer*, let alone this specific request, would have no meaning.

What is the will of God?

If we want to grasp what exactly doing God's will is, then, we can look at the second part of this petition: 'on earth as it is in heaven.' The assumption here is that God's will is done, and done perfectly, in heaven. As we saw previously, heaven is God's dwelling place. In heaven, he sits on his throne, and all of the heavenly beings carry out his will. The book of Revelation gives us a grand picture of God reigning from on high, and giving commands to all his servants. Surrounding God's throne are angelic beings, including the great seraphim, all of them courtiers ready to do God's will (Rev. 4). One function of these heavenly beings is to worship God, falling down before him and singing hymns of praise (vv. 8-11). They worship him in concert. Special praise from the myriads of angels is directed to Jesus Christ, the 'Lamb who was slain' (5:11–14). These creatures also carry out God's judgments upon the earth. There is a great deal of symbolism in this final book of the Bible.[17] Seven seals are opened by Jesus Christ, unleashing judgments and tribulations (Rev. 5:6–8:5). Seven trumpets set these judgments into motion (8:6–11:18). Seven bowls containing the wrath of God are poured out by the angels (16:1–18:24). Alongside these tribulations come the great acts of redemption, acts central to God's merciful will, also executed through his heavenly agents (7:1–17; 11:15–19; 19:1–21; 21:1–22:5).

In the West, at least that portion strongly influenced by the Enlightenment, angels don't hold much of a place in our worldview. It is altogether otherwise in the Bible. These heavenly beings are presented as those who are 'holy ones,' always doing the will of God (Deut. 33:2–3, Matt. 25:31). They are creatures of light (Acts 12:7; 2 Cor. 11:14). Daily, they behold the face of God (Matt. 18:10). Someday, we are told, believers will become like them (Luke 20:26). Accordingly, we should be mindful of their presence (1 Cor. 4:9; 11:10). We are said to preach to an angelic audience (Eph. 3:10). Together with them, we sing to the glory of God (Ps. 103:20–21).

So, in the *Lord's Prayer*, when we ask that God's will be done *as it is in heaven*, we are saying we should conform our lives to the example of the angels and other heavenly beings (Matt. 6:10). We should imitate the angels insofar as they perfectly observe God's will. If God's will is perfectly executed in heaven, it is not yet fully accomplished here on earth. Again, there is the 'already' and the 'not-yet.' So there is much left to be done. But what in particular do we seek when we ask for God's will to be done? Again, we get our cue from the angels in heaven. But here, we must pause to consider a major issue.

---

[17] For a lucid, persuasive account of the many symbols and what they represent, see Vern S. Poythress, *The Returning King: A Guide to the Book of Revelation*, Phillipsburg: P & R Publishing, 2000.

Just because angels carry out judgments does not mean we may do exactly the same. We do not extend God's kingdom though violence. There is a place for the use of force, but it is relegated to duly constituted civil authorities, not to the church, nor to individual Christians, unless they should be in the police or the armed services (Rom. 13:1-7). There are various religions which encourage violence in the name of extending their 'kingdom.' We are all familiar with recent attacks by Islamic terrorists. And throughout history numerous religions have justified purges and ritual killings. Even in certain episodes of Christian history violence has been used to advance what should be spiritual purposes. We do not have space here to examine the Crusades, but while the phenomenon of Medieval forays in the Middle East were complex in many ways, surely there was no justification for going to war in the name of Christ.[18]

If our task is not bringing judgment upon the earth, how are we to imitate the angels? The primary answer is to practice holiness. Just as the angels are holy beings, we need to ask God to cultivate such holiness in us. As we saw above, holiness is ultimately a quality of God's, designating separation: both separation from the creature (since he is the Creator) and removal from sin and evil (since he is perfect). While we as creatures will always remain creaturely, and thus can never separate from our finitude, there is a kind of separation we can engage in, and that is purity from the world. When we ask for the Lord's will to be done, we are asking God to keep us from the corruption of this present life. That is not the same as removing us altogether from the world, an impossibility. Paul explains the difference to his Corinthian readers. 'I wrote to you in my letter not to associate with sexually immoral

---

[18] Several studies on the Crusades are illuminating. The multi-volume series by Steven Runciman, *A History of the Crusades*, Cambridge; Cambridge University Press, 1987ff., is something of a classic. Régine Pernous gives a fairly balanced account of the motives and effects of the Crusades in *The Crusaders: the Struggle for the Holy Land*, Ignatius, 2003.

people—not at all meaning the sexually immoral of this world, or the greedy and swindlers, or idolaters, since then you would need to go out of the world' (1 Cor. 5:9–10). The difference is also captured in Jesus' high priestly prayer: 'I do not ask that you take them out of the world, but that you keep them from the evil one' (John 17:15).

Holiness for us means resisting any improper love for this corrupt world, and instead doing the will of God, which abides forever (1 John 2:15–17). We are thus called to take a moral stand in this world. Such a stand is the main expression of doing God's will on earth as it is in heaven. The Christian life is primarily one of following God's commandments, not out of cold duty, but because they follow, joyfully, from our transformed selves. These commandments, in a word, are not burdensome to us (1 John 5:3). One way to look into the practice of holiness is simply to examine the ten commandments. While these were first given at Mount Sinai, they have perennial significance. One can verify this because they are cited in the New Testament in terms of general principles that still apply. For example, Paul quotes four of them in Romans 13:9, and reminds his readers of the great summary of the second table of the law, 'You shall love your neighbor as yourself' (Rom. 13:9–10).

Thus, having no other gods but God, refusing to worship any creature, defending the good name of God, keeping the Sabbath, honoring authorities, refusing to murder, to commit adultery, to steal, to prevaricate, or to cultivate wrong desires, these are in fact the will of God (Ex. 20:1–17). Often, these rules are simple. At times they are not. Is it ever right to deceive? Most Christians would answer, it can be, but only in very discrete circumstances such as war. Is any form of killing murder? Most Christians would answer that the civil magistrate has the responsibility to restrain crime, even when it means preventing the criminal from living. And, in addition to following laws, such as the ten commandments, we are also enjoined to practice wisdom, which is the understanding that guides us into right actions in various circumstances.

While following the moral law is the norm for doing God's will, at times doing so can be seriously difficult. Although he was the perfect Son of God, Jesus himself agonized over doing God's will when he knew the pain and suffering it would involve at his passion. Luke records that as he prayed in the garden on the eve of his betrayal and arrest, sweat beads like blood dropped to the ground (Luke 22:44). Jesus' prayer in the Garden of Olives was itself a model of proper struggle, then resignation: 'Father, if you are willing, remove this cup from me. Nevertheless, not my will, but yours, be done' (Luke 22:42; cf. Matt. 46:39, 42). Although Jesus did die, he was then raised from the dead, because of his faithfulness to the Father's will: 'In the days of his flesh, Jesus offered up prayers and supplications, with loud cries and tears, to him who was able to save him from death, and he was heard because of his reverence' (Heb. 5:7).

Accounts of a number of believers in the Bible describe the test of their willingness to follow the will of God. We could think of Abraham, who, to test his faith, was told to sacrifice his only son (Gen. 22:1–19).[19] We could also think of Mary, the mother of Jesus, who was told that she would conceive a child as a virgin. When she asked how this might be, she was told that the Holy Spirit would come upon her. Her response: 'Behold, I am the servant of the Lord: let it be to me according to your word' (Luke 1:26–38). While humanly unbelievable, Mary knew that nothing was impossible with God. We could compare this story with the previous account of a similar announcement made to Zechariah and Elizabeth about the birth of John the Baptist. The couple was too old to have children, and so Zechariah's response was to doubt the angel's prediction. Zechariah was chastised with becoming mute until the baby was born (Luke 1:5–25, 57–66). Whereas Mary was willing from the start, Zechariah had to be convinced by being disciplined.

---

[19] He passed the test, though in the end he did not have to go through with it. The Lord was not telling him to commit murder, but to be willing to give up his first-born, permissible in the Old Testament.

Whether the challenge to obedience is fierce or not, no faithfulness to God's will is remotely possible without the grace of God. That is why we make this our prayer. We cannot obey God, or follow his will, without God's own power to do so.

Prayers

We give thanks to you, O God, for having created the world, with all things therein, for the sake of mankind; and for delivering us from the evil in which we live; and for utterly overthrowing the principalities and powers, through Him who suffered according to His will. *Amen.* (Justin Martyr, *Dialogue*, c. 150 AD)

Grant to us, Lord, we ask You, the spirit to think and do always such things as be rightful; that we, who cannot do anything that is good without You, may by You be enabled to live according to Your will; through Jesus Christ our Lord. *Amen.* (Leonine Sacramentary, c. 461 AD)

6

Give Us this Day Our Daily Bread

In the Western World we have become so accustomed to our extraordinary affluence that for many of us this petition has lost its power. That can only be because we have lost a biblical view of life. The food we eat is ours only because God upholds our universe and gives us seedtime and harvest. But beyond that, the food we eat *nourishes* us only because of his blessing (Sinclair B. Ferguson).

What are we promised?

The first three petitions, we might say, are directed toward God's chief rights and concerns: his name is hallowed, his kingdom comes and his will is done. Now we may 'descend to our own affairs,' as Calvin puts it. Not that we 'bid farewell to God's glory,' but here God allows us 'to look after our own interests, yet under this limitation: that we seek nothing for ourselves without the intention that whatever benefits he confers upon us may show forth his glory, for nothing is more fitting than that we live and die for him (Rom. 14:7-9).'[1]

---

[1] John Calvin, *Institutes of the Christian Religion* 3.20.44.

What, then, are our own proper interests? The gospel being our foundation, does that mean every Christian should expect to become wealthy? Or even that they should all exist at a subsistence level? Evidently not. When we pray for daily bread, several things need to be kept in mind. The most obvious is the assumption that God indeed listens to us and knows of our needs. But those needs fall within a larger picture, where the Lord orders our lives according to the priorities of his good Providence. Remember that the *Lord's Prayer*, or any prayer for that matter, is in itself a statement of covenant relationship between God and his people. God has promised to provide everything we need. As has already been pointed out, the thing we need most is to live in God's kingdom and to glorify and enjoy the fellowship of the king forever. So, then, how does our daily bread fit within this grand scheme?

A little later in the sermon, Jesus spoke more specifically about God's priorities, and he did so precisely in the context of our worries about food and clothing (Matt. 6:25–33). The key admonition here is 'Seek first the kingdom of God and his righteousness...' (6:33). Here is the main concern throughout. God of course promises to make his kingdom spread. But then the complete sentence reads, '*and* all these things will be added to you.' Being a priority does not mean nothing else matters. With considerable compassion, the Lord explains how the heavenly Father knows we need food and shelter and raiment (v. 32). He admonishes his disciples not to be anxious about them, as proof that the Father cares about such things he finds illustrations from the creation. The birds do not toil the way humans do to produce food, and yet they are provided for (v. 26). The lilies of the field don't set themselves to making textiles, yet the greatest king in the Old Testament, with thousands of people working for him, did not possess such simple beauty as the fields full of flowers (vv. 28–29). If this is how God provides for his non-human creation, how much more will he provide for us.

Martin Luther's *Smaller Catechism* gives a fairly extensive list of what is covered under the fourth petition: '*What is meant by daily bread?*—Answer: Everything that belongs to the support and wants of the body, such as meat, drink, clothing, shoes, house, homestead, field, cattle, money, goods, a pious spouse, pious children, pious servants, pious and faithful magistrates, good government, good weather, peace, health, discipline, honor, good friends, faithful neighbors, and the like.'

Why, then, is there deprivation? It would be cruel, and unbiblical, to say that deprivation comes from lack of faith. While faith is crucial, it is not a push-button to access God. Faith is not like a coin to put into a vending machine. The simple answer to the question 'why deprivation?' is that we live in a fallen world, and one of the consequences of the fall is deficiency in every area, including food, clothing and shelter. The gospel remedies all of these deficiencies but in God's timing and in his way. One of my favorite negro spirituals begins, 'God don't come when you want him to, but he's always right on time.' When we have this kind of faith, then we can better understand God's way of providing. When we pray, 'give us this day our daily bread,' we fully understand God's generosity, but we also fully understand his priorities, and his timing. Sometimes, the reason we must wait is that we would not understand God's ways were he to provide exactly as we think he should.

Dostoyevsky's novel, *The Brothers Karamazov*, is a tale of the temptation to patricide in a country mired by tyranny and revolt. The pernicious atheist, Ivan Karamazov, explains to his godly brother, Alyosha, that Christ made a monumental mistake. He refused to turn stones into bread. 'But see You these stones in this parched and barren wilderness? Turn them into bread, and mankind will run after You like a flock of sheep, grateful and obedient, though forever trembling, lest You withdraw Your hand and deny them your bread.' The old Cardinal in Ivan's parable of Jesus' return to a Spanish town in the sixteenth century argues that by refusing the three temptations of the devil, while he may have preached about human freedom, he could never convince the masses of people that liberty is greater than food. Freedom comes with a price. The price of self-sacrifice, faith and personal effort is far too high for them. As head of the Inquisition the Cardinal imprisons Jesus, finding his message of freedom a threat to the system.

Chapter V, Section 5, 'The Grand Inquisitor,' has become one of the great parables of the human condition. One cannot but be moved by Ivan's revolt against evil, and even his sense that a good God could not have allowed such cruelty as the death of a child. Why, if he existed, would he not first and foremost alleviate the human condition? But then Dostoyevsky invites us to take that question to its extreme. If all we need is food and clothing, then what of life's meaning? What of moral considerations? Is there any point to a life without meaning or morals?

Among other things the parable accurately predicted the tyranny of Communism in the twentieth century. Karl Marx, the major philosophical force behind Communism, taught that '... the first premise of all human existence and, therefore, of all history [is that] men must be in a position to live in order to be able to "make history". But life involves before everything else eating and drinking, a habitation, clothing and many other things.'[2] Before everything? Jesus taught the contrary. When faced with Satan's temptation to turn stones into bread, he quoted Scripture: 'Man shall not live by bread alone' (Luke 4:4). The rest of the Old Testament passage continues, 'but man lives by every word that comes from the mouth of the Lord' (Deut. 8:3).

So, then, what are we promised? The exact meaning of this petition in the *Lord's Prayer* could be, as many scholars believe, 'give us today tomorrow's bread.' In that case, we are asking

---

[2] Karl Marx & Frederick Engels, *The German Ideology*, Pt 1, New York: International publishers, 1947, 48.

God to provide for all of our needs, right up until the end. These are blessings for the last days, and we ask that they be given now (1 Cor. 10:11).[3] In an astonishing statement, the apostle Paul answers: 'So let no one boast in men. *For all things are yours*, whether Paul or Apollos or Cephas or the world or life or death or the present or the future—all are yours, and you are Christ's, and Christ is God's' (1 Cor. 3:21-23). Whereas the Corinthians had been divided over party allegiances, Paul explains to them that everything in the universe is theirs, not just the teachings of these missionaries, but life and death, the present and the future. Because, he goes on, if they are Christ's, and Christ is God's, then there is nothing outside of God's own rule that is not in some way the possession of his people (cf. 15:27, 24ff.). To want one thing to the point of jealously is to misunderstand God's generosity. This is something akin to the elder brother in the story of the 'Prodigal Son' (misnamed, since there are two sons, and since the Father is the most prodigal of all). When the penitent prodigal returns and the father throws him a large feast, the elder brother complains that he had been obedient all his life but never had a feast for himself. To which the father responded, 'Son, you are always with me, and all that is mine is yours' (Luke 15:31). So, what are we promised? Everything!

If this be the case, then, why do we not appear to have all things? Why are Christians, as well as millions of others, struggling with poverty? Certainly not because it is somehow good for us to be deprived. While a few may be called to live with few possessions, there is no biblical injunction for a life of poverty. It is important to catch the balance here. The Christian religion is not one of asceticism and deprivation. God wants his creatures to be provided for. Indeed, one of the possible signs of God's blessing is material prosperity. Abraham was a wealthy man (Gen. 13:2). So was Solomon (2 Chron. 1:12). So was Job (Job 1:3). Jesus was buried in the tomb of a wealthy

---

[3] It is not wrong to translate, 'daily,' but perhaps a bit vague.

friend, Joseph of Arimathea (Mark 15:43). Everything in creation, including possessions, money, property, are good, when received with thanksgiving (1 Tim. 4:4). However, a line is crossed when these good things become the first things. The case of Solomon is instructive. A man of extraordinary wealth, he began well, but ended in corruption and cynicism. The narrative tells us that it was his wives who lured him away into idolatry (1 Kings 11:4). We must take this account at face value. But we can imagine as well that he set himself up for such temptations by forgetting the God who at first had given him not only wealth but wisdom.

On top of that, food without God is meaningless. That is why the prophets remind us that victuals without the presence of the Lord do not satisfy (Mic. 6:14). Indeed, how many tables have an abundance of food but no real contentment?

So, where is the balance between rightful ownership of good things and idolatry? There is no simple formula or rule that covers all situations. Yet, no question but that the Christian faith is deeply concerned about finding the right balance. Our Lord insisted over and over that the poor must be a priority. The apostle Paul, along with the other apostles, had the poor uppermost in their minds as they ministered (Gal. 2:10; Rom. 15: 26). But there is a larger context, a total set of priorities which includes more than poverty relief.

Poverty

Today, there are some sobering facts to consider. Of the world population of a little over 7 billion, some 1.1 billion subsist below the internationally accepted extreme poverty line ($1.25 per day—not very much at that). Half the people of the world live on less than $2.50 per day. Fully two and a half billion are without access to proper sanitation. There are about two billion children in the world, and half of them live in poverty; that is, every second child in the world is poor. Well over one billion do not have adequate access to water. Nearly half the people of the world who live in developing countries suffer from diseases associated with poor sanitation and impure water.

These may appear to be merely numbers. But consider that behind each statistic is a person, a deeply suffering person, one of God's image-bearers in agony. Behind every impoverished family there is a story, a story of deprivation, pain, hunger, and disease. Anyone who has visited a war zone, such as Biafra in Nigeria, or areas prone to flooding, such as those extending from eastern Uttar Pradesh to the Assam plains, and especially in northern Bihar, in India, can testify to the excruciating poverty, seen in bloated bellies or desperate faces.

Poverty brings with it more than lack of subsistence, though that is one of the greatest effects. There is usually more sickness among the poor, not only because of factors such as malnutrition, but because of lack of access to health care. Also, there is likely to be less protection, and more crime in poor areas. Education is often severely lacking as well. Basically, the poor are disempowered, having little access to institutions, to legal representation, and thus have limited ability to have their aspirations for improvement succeed.

There is no one cause of poverty. Many (non-poor) assume that most poor people somehow have themselves to blame. They refused to work, or were consistently laid-off because of poor job performance, or perhaps tried a wrong-headed scheme which did not work. Undoubtedly such cases exist (Prov. 19:15). But much of the world's dire poverty is not the result of indolence or poor choices. Rather it comes from scores of causes, including, most often, various kinds of oppression from tyrants. Such causes can be found nearly anywhere, even in relatively well-to-do countries.

One often finds poverty in urban areas. The way power is exercised in the city explains in part how there could be so many who are poor, particularly in certain parts of town. Immigrants from places where the rich exploit the population, resulting in the loss of jobs, come to the cities of the more developed countries hoping to find such work. What they find there is that power in the city is held by the few, and often these few have little real interest in relieving poverty. Poor sections of town that may have grown up as temporary housing become unintentionally permanent. Scarce work, inadequate housing, and little representation, rather than opportunity, is what they find. There are, to be sure, many exceptions. My family is from New York, where a number of immigrants find work in such settings as textiles, driving taxis, waiting on tables, etc. Many times they are able to raise families and see their children succeed in ways unimaginable in their home countries.

Poverty can also be found in the countryside. Rural poverty is frequently connected with lack of infrastructure: not enough roads, phone lines, etc. Jobs are far away, education is scarce. Lack of access to markets also causes poverty. Whether because the infrastructure is not there, or because of lack of information, or, especially, lack of training, the poor are barred from having capital. When they do hold jobs, the work is often in tenant farming, care-working, or herding. The jobs are fragile, either because they are seasonal or because employers provide few guarantees such as contracts. Health benefits are often non-existent. The globalization of markets often means rural people cannot access the international sales that benefit the business elite.

Poverty does not just happen. Poverty is the result of living in a fallen world. Humanity's primary alienation from God leads inextricably to alienation at every level. Not only the poor, but all people are alienated. Yet the poor's alienation is particularly observable. The poor are far more likely to be victims of injustice than the rich. There are all kinds of reforms which would help reverse these trends. We will describe just a few of them below. But because poverty begins with alienation at every level, such alienation must be remedied. Since the primary alienation is between human beings and God, their Creator, reconciliation with him is primordial. The good news, the gospel, is that Jesus

Christ, God's only Son, became poor so that we could have all the riches we need.

We can, to be sure, note some progress. In the previous decades the number of people living beneath the poverty line has decreased significantly. If you define 'extreme poverty' as living on less than $1.25 per day, then that number has been reduced by one half since 1990.[4] An extraordinary achievement! Governments as well as Christian relief groups have multiplied their efforts and we can see significant progress in many places. Organizations such as Compassion International and World Vision have done pioneering work in providing not only relief but education and plans for sustainability. Alongside these ministries, we find NGOs who can help to some extent. Indeed, some political leaders find themselves boastfully predicting the end of poverty by the year 2030. Former British prime Minister Tony Blair said, 'We do have an historic opportunity to make poverty history.' And South Africa's president Thabo Mbeki said, 'for the first time in human history, society has the capacity, the knowledge and the resources to eradicate poverty.'[5] Having said that, great caution should be urged before accepting such predictions at face value.

Always with you?

Here, we might introduce a troubling subject. In response to criticism by the disciples of the woman who anointed him with precious oil, to the effect that the money it could have fetched would have helped alleviate poverty, Jesus told his disciples, 'For you always have the poor with you, but you will not always have me' (Matt. 26:11; Mark 14:7; see John 12:8). This is actually a near quote from Deuteronomy 15:11. On the surface

---

[4] [http://web.worldbank.org/WBSITE/EXTERNAL/TOPICS/
EXTPOVERTY/EXTPA/0,,contentMDK:20040961~menuPK:435040~pag
ePK:148956~piPK:216618~theSitePK:430367~isCURL:Y,00.html]

[5] 'Not always with Us,' *The Economist*, June 1–7, 2013, 407/8838, 21.

this kind of statement appears to be downplaying, or at least relativizing the plight of the poor. Is Jesus here being somewhat callous, or is there another explanation? I once heard a sermon about the Christian approach to social reform saying that there is no real hope for change in the world, and we simply need to concentrate on the needs of the church, particularly our church. These passages were cited to support the view that we simply do not have the resources to combat world poverty and world hunger, but that perhaps we had enough in-house resources to take care of the local Christian poor.

First, this interpretation would make no sense in view of the countless places in Scripture where we are enjoined to combat poverty. Throughout the Old Testament there are plentiful commands to work hard to relieve poverty. To begin with, the very passage Jesus paraphrased from Deuteronomy 15 should be quoted in full: 'For there will never cease to be poor in the land. Therefore I command you, "You shall open wide your hand to your brother, to the needy and to the poor, in your land." The sequence here is, because there will be poor people in your land you will constantly need to be vigilant and reach out to them. So at the very least, Jesus is not saying, because there will always be the poor, you cannot do much about it.

Second, insouciance toward the poor is a major symptom of a country's social illness. According to many of the prophets oppressing the poor is a sign of decadence, and liability to judgment. 'What do you mean by crushing my people,' the Lord says through Isaiah, 'by grinding the face of the poor?' (Isa. 3:15). Isaiah's prophecy is replete with accusations of insensitivity to the poor and needy. The connection between poverty and injustice is made throughout the Scriptures. Consider the tragic incident of King David's adultery with Bathsheba and the murder of her husband (2 Sam. 11:1–12:23). While David was living in his complacency, the Lord sent Nathan the prophet to speak to him about his guilt. Instead of reading him the riot act he told a story. There was a rich man with many herds of sheep and cattle who wanted to entertain a traveling guest with a lamb dinner. Yet instead of using one of his own sheep for the feast, he went and stole the one ewe lamb from a poor man's bosom. Nathan begins the story by saying 'There were two men in a certain city, the one rich and the other poor' (12:1). Throughout, the two are named 'rich' and 'poor.' At the end of the story, David is incensed and tells Nathan the rich man deserves to die and that he would make him pay. Although the main point of the story is to appeal to what remained of David's conscience after his gross misconduct, it is not without significance that the two main characters are a rich man and a poor man. Nathan's story is not a Grimm *Fairy Tale* where we feel sorry for Cinderella because she is maligned (although there is, to be sure, a remote connection), but one infused with the Jewish sense of the full evil of poverty.

So then, third, what exactly is Jesus telling his disciples? Consider the setting for his statement. A woman came to Jesus with an alabaster jar full of the most precious ointment, and poured it over his head. She was, as Jesus explains, memorializing his body, preparing it for burial. What a remarkable insight! She understood the gospel. She understood that unless Jesus died there could be no redemption for sinners. As such not only was he worthy of being memorialized, but of being worshiped. Because she understood this, she would be remembered wherever the gospel would be preached. As right here! Judas had suggested this expensive ointment could have been sold and given to the poor. As we know, and Jesus knew then, Judas' motives were hardly compassionate. He was a materialist, not particularly concerned for the poor but for the cost-effectiveness of the woman's gesture. Jesus rebukes him.

Jesus is hardly unconcerned for the poor as his entire life demonstrated. Even here he reminds them, 'whenever you want, you can do good for them' (Mark 14:7). But he wanted his disciples to understand, as this woman so clearly had, that his presence, his teaching, his healing, and all that his incarnation represented, is of even greater value than the immediate relief of the poor. In effect, he is saying, there will be plenty of opportunities for poverty relief, which you should be busy accomplishing. But there will be few opportunities to benefit from *my* presence, to understand *my* ministry, and to contemplate the implications of *my* life on earth, then *my* death and resurrection. The shepherds understood this at Jesus' birth. And so did the Magi. Only when life has become completely commoditized can such generosity be denied.

Having said that, this statement of Jesus, quoting Deuteronomy 15, does tell us something sobering. However much progress we may make, world poverty is with us and will always be with us until the end. That is no excuse either for resignation or complacency, but it does highlight the crushing reality and the tenacity of poverty. About this our Lord was a realist.

Praying, and sharing

We must ask ourselves two questions. First, what can the poor do? Second, what can those who have more means do? Poor people have few resources. But they do have some. In certain parts of the world disenfranchised people show resilience. A number of studies have shown that the most likely predictors of resilience include strong family ties, a certain work ethic, small victories such as finding a supportive institution or watching children grow into responsible adulthood. Most often it is when there is a strong sense of purpose, usually connected with religion, particularly biblical religion.[6] For example, various churches in poor regions of Uganda have organized to provide medical care, grain storage rooms, tree-planting and micro-credit loans to the populations.[7]

---

[6] See for example, E. E. Werner, & R. S. Smith, *Journeys from Childhood to Midlife: Risk, Resiliency, and Recovery*. Ithaca, NY: Cornell University Press, 2001; and Donald Robertson, *Resilience*, London: Hodder & Stoughton, 2012.

[7] One of many examples is the Micah Network, sponsored by the Assemblies of God [http://www.micahnetwork.org/sites/default/files/doc/library/church_and_community_development_pag_uganda.pdf].

So, then, how does prayer, and particularly the petition for daily bread, function in relation to such actions? Is that perfunctory? No. 'Give us this day our daily bread' is not simply a pious acknowledgement that God is somehow behind our being fed. Rather it should be the desperate plea of his people: 'Lord, if you do not feed me, I shall go hungry.' Throughout Scripture we witness a consciousness about the need for God's generosity if there is to be any nourishment. 'For he satisfies the longing soul, and the hungry soul he fills with good things,' the Psalmist tells us (Ps. 107:9). This is not only true for human beings, but for the entire creation (Ps. 104:27). If we do ask the Father, Jesus tells us, how shall he give us a stone instead of bread, or a serpent instead of a fish? (Matt. 7:9-10) Food does not just come to the table. We often hear that somewhat awkward grace, thanking God 'for the hands that prepared it.' But were not God at work, there would be no food at all, nor hands to prepare it. Not enough food? Pray. Too much food and no God? Pray.

Such a prayer only makes sense if we understand God's special concern for the hungry and oppressed. Psalm 9 tells us, 'The Lord is a stronghold for the oppressed,' and that 'The needy shall not always be forgotten' (vv. 9, 18). Psalm 2 declares that 'the afflicted shall eat and be satisfied' (v. 26). Throughout we are reminded that God will deliver the afflicted and the hungry (Ps. 72:4, 12-14; 102:17; 107:9; 113:7; Isa. 14:30; 25:5; Ezek. 16:49). To be sure, the timing of God's answer is crucial. Patently he does not fill the hungry with food in every place, nor does he do so immediately. How then is this prayer still valid? As we saw earlier, this is where faith must come in. It may be that in this life many are called to be in want. While this is a great hardship, it does not abrogate the meaning of this prayer. After all, we are asking God to provide our daily bread, not telling him when and how to do it. While such faith is not bitter resignation it does not mean a forced happiness, when this part of life is anything but comfortable.

At the same time we see throughout Scripture that those with some means have a strong responsibility to help out.

Whether they are insiders or come from outside, those with ability are enjoined to come and help those without.

Sufficient resources?

While it is certainly the case that various agencies and institutions can be of help, our primary concern here is to remind Christian believers of their responsibilities. The question we must raise, though, is whether the church has the resources to give such help? We sometimes hear sermons that answer in the negative. They may agree to helping the local poor, but declare that there should be no involvement in any larger programs aiming to eradicate world-wide poverty. We must respectfully disagree. The church does have the resources, although those resources do not always reach the needy as they should. When Christ ascended on high he poured out gifts to his people (Eph. 4:8). While there are gifts of all kinds, including 'spiritual' gifts such as teaching and pastoral leadership, other gifts include resources for all of life. Christ has given, and is giving his church all that she needs. But that does not mean every congregation has every gift. This is certainly true in the realm of finance. Because every congregation is in the same 'communion of the saints' with every other congregation there should be mutual benefit. Those who have a great deal should sense a responsibility for those who have less.

We see this principle at work in the New Testament times. The apostle Paul often refers to a money offering in cultic terms. One of the most significant offerings recorded is based not only on the principle of available resources but on the metaphor of worship. The apostle Paul gathers moneys from various churches for the purpose of relief to the church at Jerusalem. Romans 15 alludes to the coming into the kingdom of the Gentiles. At one point Paul refers to the 'offering of the Gentiles,' that is, most likely, the offering given by the Gentiles as members of the New Testament churches (15:16). That offering is destined for Jerusalem not only for relief but because of the significance of that city for worship.[8] The same is true of Paul's appeal to the Corinthian church to store up the offering for Jerusalem before he arrives in Corinth (1 Cor. 16:1-4).

When pleading to the Corinthians to give generously for the cause of the needy Christians in Jerusalem, Paul made the essential argument that all of us, once poor, are now rich in God's grace. And because of this we all ought to be generous to others in need. How were we made rich in grace? By the sacrifice of our redeemer. 'For you know the grace of our Lord Jesus Christ, that though he was rich, yet for your sake he became poor, so that by his poverty you might become rich' (2 Cor. 8:9).

While certainly a formal ministry or 'diaconal program' should characterize the church, much ministry of mercy ought to go on at an informal level. When church members learn to 'see' their neighbor in need, without prompting, they go into action at the level of their ability. The parable of the Good Samaritan (Luke 10:25-37) illustrates this principle. 'And who is my neighbor?' the lawyer asked Jesus, no doubt wanting to set up a grid of eligible or ineligible candidates for neighborly obligation. 'Who qualifies for my charity?' he was asking. We can guess that the spirit of this request was minimalist: I know I should help some people, but the fewer the better. Famously Jesus answered with what has become one of the great classics in literature. A man is robbed and left for dead. A priest, then a Levite saw it but passed by, not stopping. 'But a certain Samaritan,' in the King James Version, 'as he journeyed, came where he was: and when he saw him, he had compassion on him' (v. 33). He administered first aid, took him to an inn, paid for him, left, saying when he returned he would pay any leftover bills.

---

[8] An excellent study of the Jerusalem offering is David J. Downs, *The Offering of the Gentiles: Paul's Collection for Jerusalem in Its Chronological, Cultural and Cultic Contexts*, Tübingen: Mohr-Siebeck, 2008.

Jesus then brings an important twist to the story. Instead of answering the lawyer's question the way it was formulated, he asked, 'Which of these three, do you think, proved to be a neighbor to the man who fell among the robbers?' (v. 36). The lawyer wanted a list of neighbors who qualified for aid. Instead, what he really needed was to determine whether he was a compassionate sort or not. 'The one who showed him mercy' was the only right answer. He is then told to go and do likewise. Of course the victim was a neighbor, a neighbor in need. But only if we ourselves are 'neighborly' by virtue of our compassionate heart, are we really living in the kingdom.

How can we develop such neighborly compassion? By gazing upon Jesus. The Samaritan in the story is a hated outsider. But he did the right thing. Jesus, the hated outsider, did the right thing. Out of his compassion he came, died for us, and fully paid the price for our redemption. We may now live in a safe haven because he showed mercy. Only when we grasp the enormous cost of our redemption, driven by Jesus' fathomless love, can we begin to turn around and see who is in need, and respond. Only when we develop a neighbor's heart, can we engage in the ministry of mercy. Because only when we have a neighbor's heart can we actually recognize a person in need and go and help.

Christians ought to develop neighborly relationships. That may be difficult for some people. They are fearful, shy, etc. But, driven by the love of Christ, they will be on the lookout for neighbors in need. My wife, Barbara, is much better at these things than I. She will buy extra groceries and drop them off to someone who needs them. She tutors a teenager across the street who struggles with his school. She is constantly on the phone with elderly people who are homebound. Notice how such neighborliness can occur anywhere, in the country, in the suburbs, in the city.

From relief to reform

So, where do we begin? New York pastor Timothy Keller makes a suggestion about how to order our priorities in order to address all of the problems and not simply a few of them.[9] Intervention should move from *relief*, through *transformation*, to *reform*, he affirms. First, when there is a crying need for food, for shelter, for first aid, there should be relief: direct assistance to alleviate that condition. So, when someone comes to the church destitute, some sort of immediate relief is appropriate. Giving money outright is delicate. Usually it is best to find out exactly what the person's condition is before monetary donations are appropriate. Also, in almost all circumstances, there needs to be some counseling and provision for instruction in how to handle problems. Often, people with dire needs are struggling with drugs, child rearing, divorce, grieving, sickness, and the like. At this point referrals may be appropriate as well (temporary housing, medical care, nutrition centers).

Second, relief should never be proffered without at least some consideration for transformation. This does not mean compassion should be conditional. Just as God's love is unconditional, so should ours be. But real love will include provisions for the long term. Even more than with relief, transformation will require educational training, employment opportunities, housing, and the like.

Only when these approaches are beginning to be in place can one talk of the third step: reform. Reform comes when policy makers can be moved to make improvements. Keller says, 'This means a church must get to know the policy-making leaders of the community and must learn how to disseminate information to them. This is no less than social reform, and the church of Jesus Christ is bound to do it.'[10] Of course, the church as an institution is one aspect of the church, and the church as a community of believers is another. In some countries the only institution with any clout is the church, just as the only leaders with any education are clergy. In other countries where the church is but one of several institutions with clout then

---

[9] *Ministries of Mercy*, op. cit., 180ff.

[10] Ibid., 188.

individual Christians may do more to effect reform. A judge may be a believer and will take his or her office to be divinely appointed, and thus obliged to make changes based on biblical principles. A lawmaker may be a Christian, and will seek the most just and equitable policies in that sphere. A school administrator may be a follower of Christ and will endeavor to enact educational reform. Or, one can think of the great reform movements in history, such as the abolition of slavery, curtailing child labor, women's suffrage, etc.

True contentment

Going back to our very first question. What are we promised? The answer to that, as we saw, is: an awful lot! But all in due time. Now, then comes the next question. When we pray, 'give us this day our daily bread,' what are we striving for, at least here and now? Obviously poverty must be addressed, and destitution combated. But how about the other end? How much is too much? Of course there is no blueprint for Christian wealth management. And there is room for variety here. The Proverbs are full of wisdom about handling money. Generally they strive for a careful balance.

> Two things I ask of you;
> Deny them not to me before I die:
> Remove far from me falsehood and lying;
> Give me neither poverty nor riches;
> feed me with the food that is needful for me,
> lest I be full and deny you
> and say, 'Who is the Lord?'
> or lest I be poor and steal
> and profane the name of my God. (Prov. 30:7-9)

While it would be a stretch to move from this teaching to an endorsement of a middle-class Christianity, as some have done, the idea that Christians should neither have too much nor too little has much to commend itself.[11] Too much can lead to corruption, as we saw in the case of Solomon. When Jesus spoke of the seductions of 'mammon,' he was using a term from the Aramaic signifying wealth, or possessions as an ultimate (Matt. 6:24). Often, when we have too much wealth, we begin to be drawn to it in an unhealthy way, until it begins to claim our service. We will need to choose. But, how much is too much? To be sure, there are no fixed rules here. But a case can be made for 'small is beautiful.' The French sociologist Jacques Ellul once admitted that he kept just enough money to live, and then gave the rest away. The sobering reality is that many rich people deny God. Few of us actually request of God that he not give us too much! But it is a reasonable request, considering what can happen.

Too little can also be a great problem. There is nothing romantic about poverty. While Marxism spoke of the greatness of the proletarian class, in practice it could never really respect it. Besides, poor people can be as unjust as anyone else. In the Old Testament the judge was instructed not to favor the poor without reason (Ex. 23:3; Lev. 19:15). In desperation, the poor can be driven to steal, which is never commended. Indeed, laws against theft are abundant throughout the Bible. We can steal people, as in the despicable practice of 'man-stealing' and slave-trading (1 Tim. 1:10; Ex. 21:16; Deut. 24:7). We can also steal hearts. Jacob is said to have stolen Laban's heart when he took his wives and his possessions (Gen. 31:20–26). Absalom 'stole the hearts' of the people of Israel, setting them against his father David (2 Sam. 15:6). We can extend this to the propaganda speeches of Hitler or Stalin, or anyone else who twists the truth in order to steal, or manipulate, the thoughts of

[11] Deriving from such texts justification for a permanent middle class runs the danger of denying the way culture is dynamic, needing to strive for justice, rather than trying to conform to some 'natural' ideal. See, Ryan C. McIlhenney, 'Christian Witness As Redeemed Culture,' *Kingdoms Apart*, Ryan C. McIlhenny, ed., Phillipsburg: P & R Publishing, 2012, 262–263.

the people. Theft can also be the simple act of taking property from another. Hardly the exclusive domain of poor people, kings and rulers can steal and get away with it more often than the destitute. Stealing, though, a breach of the eighth commandment, is among other things a declaration of not being content. Ultimately, it says, God is not providing for me.

Having enough to be content is something of a biblical ideal. The apostle Paul writes: 'Let the thief no longer steal, but rather let him labor, doing honest work with his own hands, so that he may have something to share with anyone in need' (Eph. 4:28). As is his custom, Paul begins with a negative: steal no longer. But then he rushes back with a positive: work with your own hands. He does not finish there, though, because he adds a greater kingdom purpose: so as to give to those in need.

The rather elaborate commentary on the fourth petition in the *Westminster Larger Catechism* explains, among other things, that '[we] may, of his free gift, and as to his fatherly wisdom shall seem best, enjoy a competent portion of them; and have the same continued and blessed unto us in our holy and comfortable use of them, and contentment in them; and be kept from all things that are contrary to our temporal support and comfort.'[12] Francis Schaeffer begins his classic study on the Christian life with the ten commandments, stressing the last one, the 'inward' law of not coveting. He suggests two basic tests to help us decide whether we are on the road to true spirituality. The first is, do I know contentment. If I love God enough to be contented, then I am free from covetousness. The second is, do I love my neighbor enough not to envy?[13]

J. Douma, in his excellent study of the ten commandments, asks this intriguing question. Can we be too generous?[14] He

---

[12] *Westminster Larger Catechism* Q. & A. 193.

[13] *True Spirituality*, op. cit., 7–17.

[14] J. Douma, *The Ten Commandments: Manual for the Christian Life*, Nelson D. Kloosterman, trans., Phillipsburg: P & R Publishing,1996, 306.

continues, if we could give everything away, and make many people give, that would only ease a tiny bit of global suffering. 'Can we enjoy with an honest and quiet conscience what we have left over after deducting our donations for various worthwhile causes?' His answer is that after sacrificial giving it is quite all right to enjoy the wealth God has given us, 'without a bitter aftertaste.' Douma cites the feasts in the Old Testament, and Jesus' example of attending a wedding in Cana. There is a time to be shocked by world poverty, and there is a time simply to enjoy going on holiday.[15]

Spiritual food

There is more to the petition, 'Give us this day our daily bread,' than economics and the provision of food. Or, put differently, food is a real need, but it is also a metaphor for spiritual nourishment. Jacques Ellul, again, makes the connection:

> The only attitude that Christianity can require is personal commitment. We must take personal responsibility for the state of the poor; this is being responsible before God. But we are entering dangerous territory. We must not sweeten the gospel to make it acceptable. All we can do is measure our faith against the Word spoken to us, God's question which puts our life in question. To accept our responsibility is to enter into the spiritual and material condition of those who put God's question to the world. It is, in fact, to become poor ourselves with the poor, with the Poor One.[16]

When we give, as when we receive, we are participating in the larger realm of 'God's question.' That is, we face God and render account to him from our hearts. Are we the 'poor in spirit' of the Sermon on the Mount, rich in faith and heirs of

[15] Ibid., 307.
[16] Jacques Ellul, *Money and Power*, Eugene, OR: Wipf & Stock, 2009, 160.

the kingdom? (Matt. 5:3; James 2:5) Or are we the oppressive rich who blaspheme the name of the Lord? (James 2:6–7)

Only if we are truly submitted to God through Jesus Christ can we hope to have the right sustenance, both physically and spiritually. Yet, as the insight from Jacques Ellul shows, a just use of property reflects the larger picture of our standing before God's Word, and, indeed, before God himself. The *Heidelberg Catechism* captures this relationship well:

> Q. What is the fourth petition?
>
> A. 'Give us this day our daily bread.' That is: be pleased to provide for all our bodily needs so that thereby we may acknowledge that thou art the only source of all that is good, and that without thy blessing neither our care and labor nor thy gifts can do us any good. Therefore we may withdraw our trust from all creatures and place it in thee alone. (Lord's Day 50, Q. & A. 125)

The Bible does not divide life up into the spiritual and the profane. The fundamental point of having food and other good provided is so that we may turn our hearts toward the giver. Our working for them is fine, but without God's blessing, these efforts are futile.

The entirety of chapter six of John's Gospel is an account of the relationship between Jesus Christ and the bread of life. The first portion is the story of the feeding of the five thousand. With only a small boy's five barley loaves and two fish, Jesus fed five thousand people. So impressed was the crowd, they sought to make him their king (6:15). He refused, and instead withdrew to a lone mountain. After walking to his disciples on water and landing his boat on the other side of the sea of Tiberias, the next day the amazed crowds tried to explain his disappearance, and to find him, which they finally did. Jesus told them all they really wanted was more food, and he urged them to labor 'for the food that endures to eternal life' (vv. 26–27). This he could provide. Not clear on the difference between the sign and the spiritual reality, the crowd wanted bread, like the Manna from heaven, when Jesus explained to them that what they needed was 'the bread of God' (v. 33). 'I am the bread of life,' he declared, adding, 'whoever comes to me shall not hunger, and whoever believes in me shall never thirst' (v. 35).

There follows a rich discourse on the Father sending the Son to gather up his own and raise them up on the last day (vv. 37–51). Intertwined with this teaching about belonging to God is the food metaphor:

> Truly, truly, I say to you, whoever believes has eternal life. I am the bread of life. Your fathers ate the manna in the wilderness, and they died. This is the bread that comes down from heaven, so that one may eat of it and not die. I am the living bread that came down from heaven. If anyone eats of this bread, he will live forever. And the bread that I will give for the life of the world is my flesh (6:47-51).

Here Jesus speaks of his becoming nourishment to believers. Having descended from heaven in order to sacrifice his own flesh, he gives us life in a way the earthly manna described in Exodus 16 and Numbers 11 could never do. This life-giving 'bread' from Jesus is the only kind really worth laboring for, since it is imperishable (vv. 27, 41).

The temptation is strong to connect these words with the sacrament of the Lord's Supper, as several commentators have done. True, talk of the bread of life being compared to Jesus' flesh could be interpreted sacramentally. Especially since the words of institution for the Lord's Supper include, 'Take, eat, this is my body' (Matt. 26:26; Mark 14:22; Luke 22:18; cf. 1 Cor. 11:24). But the reference in verse 51 is to Christ's incarnation, and the continued nourishment that Jesus' gift of his flesh would provide. So, while the passage is not anti-sacramental, what is in view here is far broader. No doubt the Lord's Supper is a beautiful application of this discourse, but not the other way around.[17] 'What Jesus maintains here... is nothing less than the surrender to death of the flesh and blood of the Son of man and the (believing) 'eating' and 'drinking' of it as the bread that came down from heaven by which alone a human being can live (v. 50)'.[18] Even in eternity God's people will be fed by the heavenly manna (see Rev. 2:17).

Jesus gives a very specific kind of nourishment to his people. Luke's version of the *Lord's Prayer* is followed by the discourse on the 'friend at midnight' (Luke 11:5-13). A man asks his reluctant neighbor for food. He finally gives in because of his perseverance. Jesus then encourages his disciples to ask of God, and he, who is hardly reluctant, will give it to them (v. 9). Then follows a passage, parallel to the one in Matthew, which instructs them to ask, to seek, and to knock (Matt. 7:7-11). Whereas in Matthew, the last phrase says, 'If you then, who are evil, know how to give good gifts to your children, how much more will your Father who is in heaven give good things to those who ask him!' (v. 11), in Luke it says, '...how much more will the heavenly Father give the *Holy Spirit* to those who ask him!' (Luke 11:13).

Luke loves to present the Holy Spirit. The Spirit is omnipresent in the Lucan birth narrative (1:35, 41, 67; 2:25-6). Jesus, himself baptized by the Holy Spirit, would come baptizing with the Holy Spirit and with fire (3:16, 22). The Spirit drove Jesus into the wilderness to be tempted (4:1). He rejoiced in the Holy Spirit (10:21). When dragged up before the authorities, the Holy Spirit would give the disciples the words to say (12:10, 12). The Spirit's work is predicted in John's Gospel (John 14:26). And, not to be missed, is the Johannine version of the 'great commission,' wherein Jesus tells the disciples 'As the Father sent me, even so I am sending you,' and breathed on

---

[17] John Calvin considers this passage to be about 'the perpetual eating of faith,' which is not restricted to the Lord's Supper, although that meal is a 'seal of this discourse.' *Commentary on St John 1–10*, Grand Rapids: Eerdmans, 1995, 169.

[18] Herman Ridderbos, *The Gospel of John: A Theological Commentary*, Grand Rapids & Cambridge: Eerdmans, 1997, 240.

them so that they could receive the Holy Spirit, giving them the authority to proclaim the forgiveness of sins (20:21–23).

And then the Spirit's presence is repeatedly recounted in the Book of Acts, volume two of Luke's Gospel. There are literally hundreds of references to the presence and work of the Holy Spirit in connection with building up and sustaining the church in the first few decades. And throughout the letter, we read constantly of the Holy Spirit's role in the local and the universal church. Not only is the Spirit the *means*, but he is the very essence of the reality of God's work. Here is how Paul characterizes the kingdom of God, as he argues for brotherly tolerance over small things such as diet: 'For the kingdom of God is not a matter of eating and drinking but of righteousness and peace and joy in the Holy Spirit' (Rom 14:17).

The joy of the Lord

Joy! Our Lord, in many ways and in many places, draws attention to our dependence on him through his generous provision. Food and other nourishment are frequent images of that provision. Just as every living creature looks to God for food in due season, so he provides food and oil and wine for his human creatures (Pss. 104:14–15, 27; 136:25; Acts 14:17). More specifically, God gives his children spiritual food through his Son Jesus Christ. In the extended metaphor of the 'true vine,' Jesus tells his disciples there can be no fruit-bearing unless they be his branches (John 15:1–11).

Although he is describing the fruit of the vine, which is grapes, yet we would not divorce that fruit from its intended product, the wine it becomes. And wine in the Bible is often a picture of abundance, joyfulness, wealth. How significant it is that Jesus' very first miracle was at a wedding feast, and consisted of producing excellent wine when the master of the feast had run out. To have Jesus is to have the joy of his presence. That is why the disciples feasted while Jesus was on earth (Matt. 9:15; Luke 5:34). The time for fasting is after he is gone. But then the time to feast again is in his presence forever (Rev. 19:9). In the end, as Abraham Kuyper reminds us, as we ask for daily bread, we should be 'longing, not for God's gifts, but for God himself. As the Shulamite calls for her bridegroom, so does the praying soul, from the consuming desire of love, pray and thirst for the possession of its Maker, and to be possessed of him.'[19]

Prayer

O LORD, in whom is the source and inexhaustible fountain of all good things, pour out thy blessing upon us, and sanctify to our use the meat and drink which are the gifts of thy kindness towards us, that we, using them soberly and frugally as thou enjoinest, may eat with a pure conscience. Grant, also, that we may always both with true heartfelt gratitude acknowledge, and with our lips proclaim thee our Father and the giver of all good, and, while enjoying bodily nourishment, aspire with special longing of heart after the bread of thy doctrine, by which our souls may be nourished in the hope of eternal life, through Christ Jesus our Lord, *Amen*. (John Calvin, 'Several Godly Prayers,' appended to *Catechism of the Church of Geneva*, 1560)

---

[19] Abraham Kuyper, *The Work of the Holy Spirit*, Henri De Vries, transl., New York: Funk & Wagnals, 1900, 631.

7

And Forgive Us Our Debts
as We Forgive Our Debtors

I really must digress to tell you a bit of good news. Last week, while at prayer, I suddenly discovered—or felt as if I did—that I had really forgiven someone I have been trying to forgive for over thirty years. Trying, and praying that I might. When the thing actually happened—suddenly as the longed-for cessation of one's neighbor's radio—my feeling was 'But it's so easy. Why didn't you do it ages ago?' So many things are done easily the moment you can do them at all. But till then, sheerly impossible, like learning to swim. (C. S. Lewis)

Debts or trespasses?

As we mentioned earlier, the *King James Version* of the Bible translates, 'Forgive us our debts as we forgive our debtors,' whereas the *Book of Common Prayer* translates, 'Forgive us our trespasses as we forgive those who trespass against us.' Today, very often, Presbyterians, Methodists, and other non-Anglicans say 'debts and debtors,' whereas Anglicans, Roman Catholics and Eastern Orthodox use 'trespasses.' One ethnic joke has it that Presbyterians, from Scotland, are more comfortable with the pecuniary term, whereas the land rich Anglicans better understand encroachments on one's property! The truth is that these words translate the Greek term *opheilema*, which does carry the sense of something owed to another.[1] The Scripture represents sin in a number of ways: as falling short of the mark, as rebellion, as pollution, all of these in relation to God. Here, in the *Lord's Prayer*, the emphasis is on sins as unpaid debts. The general idea behind 'debts' is obligation. Our primary obligation is to God, but closely related is our secondary obligation, that of our neighbors who are accountable because they have somehow sinned against us. However, this term can refer both literally to money or property owed but also metaphorically to different kinds of obligations. It can be positive, as it is when Paul describes the Christian life to the Romans this way: 'So then, brothers, we are debtors, not to the flesh, to live according to the flesh... but if by the Spirit you put to death the deeds of the body, you will live' (8:12–13). Again to the Romans Paul explains how to relate to one's neighbors, using several senses of the idea of debt: 'Pay to all what is owed to them: taxes to whom taxes are owed, revenue to whom revenue is owed, respect to whom respect is owed, honor to whom honor is owed.' But it can be negative, as when he says, 'Owe no one anything, except to love each other' (13:7–8).

Sin is a many-faceted evil. The *Westminster Shorter Catechism* defines it thus: 'Sin is any want of conformity unto, or transgression of, the law of God' (Q. & A. 14). Notice how sins of omission come first, followed by sins of commission. Similarly,

---

[1] The NIV translates Luke 11:4, 'Forgive us our sins, for we also ourselves forgive everyone who sins against us.' It is more accurate (as in the KJV and the ESV) to translate, 'and forgive us our sins, for we ourselves forgive everyone who is indebted (*opheilo*) to us.'

the Anglican prayer of confession has it, 'we have left undone those things which we ought to have done, and we have done those things which we ought not to have done, and there is no health in us.' J. I. Packer comments, 'When Christians examine themselves, it is for omissions that they should first look, and they will always find that their saddest sins take the form of good left undone.'[2] The *Shorter Catechism* goes on to describe not only the guilt and corruption of sin, but its result in lack of communion with God and in misery (Q.&A. 15–19).

The remedy for this double debt, ours toward God and our neighbors' toward us, is forgiveness. That is our plea. When we sin against God, we rack up an obligation toward him. Our guilt is like a bad debt. And the account grows and grows. How will it be erased? When we offend God, we are liable to him. We owe him, but there is no way we can pay him back. As judge, as the holy one whose name we have earlier hallowed in our prayer, he cannot but hold us accountable. Put in starker terms, our sin earns us God's enmity. Not only have we made ourselves his enemies, but he must make himself ours (Rom. 5:10; 11:12). Before coming to Christ our mind was 'hostile toward God' (Col. 1:21). Paul wept because some people had become 'enemies of the cross of Christ' (Phil. 3:18).

But God has forgiven us! While we were enemies we were reconciled to him (Rom. 5:10). This is the heart of the gospel. The best-known verse in all of Scripture says it simply and powerfully: 'For God so loved the world that he gave his only Son, that whoever believes in him should not perish but have eternal life' (John 3:16). Eternal life is far more than existence forever, it is a quality of life, the life we can only have when in fellowship with God himself. This life was forfeited by our first parents, but now is offered to us as a free gift. How can we repay our debt to God? We cannot. The debt is too great and God's standards are too high. Even if we could find a way from

---

[2] J. I. Packer, *Praying the Lord's Prayer*, Wheaton: Crossway, 2007, 78.

now on to be good, which we cannot, that would still leave all our past sins unatoned for.

How could a holy God forgive the sins of believers? Only through the extraordinarily painful death of Christ. He was not spared by the Father (Rom. 8:32). And he willingly consented to this sacrifice (John 10:17–18). Dying for us, he paid the debt so that we would not have to. The *substitutionary atonement* as this is called is not a very popular doctrine these days. However, there is no other way. Unless Christ suffered the penalty of the law, and unless he fully obeyed its demands, both on our behalf, then all is lost. In one of the most extraordinary pronouncements in the New Testament, we are told, 'For our sake he [God] made him [Christ] to be sin who knew no sin, so that in him we might become the righteousness of God' (2 Cor. 5:21). Christ here is said never to have known sin. He has been tempted in every way like us, yet without yielding to sin (Heb. 4:15). 'In him there is no sin' (1 John 3:5). This sinlessness refers to Christ's incarnate state, not to his divine nature from eternity (in which, though, it goes without saying, he was always holy, without sin). Crucially, 2 Corinthians 5:21 does not say that God made him a *sinner*. That would undo all of the plan of salvation. Rather, he made him to be *sin*. According to Philip Hughes, this is how 'God the Father made His innocent incarnate Son to be the object of his wrath and judgment, for our sakes, with the result that in Christ on the cross the sin of the world is judged and taken away.'[3]

Similarly, Paul does not say that in him we might become *righteous*, but we become *the righteousness of God*. The gospel is not about renovation, but about forgiveness. Renovation follows, but that is not the heart of the gospel. Even if we should become righteous, that could hardly commend us to God, for even at our best, our righteousness is as a polluted garment (Isa. 64:6). Becoming the righteousness of God means

---

[3] *Commentary on the Second Epistle to the Corinthians*, op. cit, 213.

a God-righteousness, one which is wholly from him. Christ's spotless perfection is imputed to us by a divine declaration (Rom. 3:21–26). Christ came into the world to save sinners (1 Tim. 1:15). His mission was accomplished. When we turn to God, lifting up the empty hands of faith, he forgives us. God does not forgive us reluctantly but gladly. He pursues us relentlessly until we come to him in faith. 'As I live, declares the Lord God, I have no pleasure in the death of the wicked, but that the wicked turn from his way and live...' (Ezek. 33:11). Yes, God is merciful and gracious, slow to anger and abounding in steadfast love. Hallelujah!

Having said this, sadly, we Christians do go on sinning. The *Lord's Prayer* is not addressing unbelievers with a call to faith, although it certainly could have such an effect. The prayer is for those who are already disciples, and in need of daily forgiveness. Even though we are new creatures in Christ we still rack up debt toward God. 'If we say we have no sin,' John tells us, 'we deceive ourselves, and the truth is not in us. If we confess our sins, he is faithful and just to forgive us our sins and to cleanse us from all unrighteousness' (1 John 1:8–9). He goes on to put the matter most emphatically: 'If we say we have not sinned, we make him a liar, and his word is not in us' (v. 10). So we stand in need of daily mercy.

The tragic seriousness of sin

In his powerful and disturbing book, *Not the Way It's Supposed to Be: A Breviary of Sin*, Cornelius Plantinga wants to retrieve an 'old awareness' that has greatly diminished in our times.[4] He outlines some of the reasons we are not able to speak out frankly about sin. We tend to trivialize sin, or use such blaspheming phrases as 'this dessert is sinfully delicious.' Much of Western culture has traded-in objective moral standards for the thera-

---

[4] Cornelius Plantinga, Jr., *Not the Way It's Supposed to Be: A Breviary of Sin*, Grand Rapids: Eerdmans, 1995.

peutic: I am no longer wrong, but 'insensitive.' The book takes us through nearly two hundred pages of confrontation with the varieties of sin, from corruption to perversion to masquerade, pride, folly and addiction. Yet none of this 'breviary' is gratuitous. Throughout Plantinga offers us relief, mainly in the peace of God, the God who has overcome sin by himself being subject to its cancer. Crucially, his definition of sin is 'any act—any thought, desire, emotion, word, or deed—or its particular absence, that displeases God and deserves blame.'[5]

The point I wish to underscore is that we will never understand the gravity of sin if we begin with ourselves. However honest and even probing our self-examination, we will never come close to understanding our guilt the way it is from the divine perspective. However penetrating the inventory of our faults, if we do not begin with God, we will never quite see how grave the situation is. How do we do that? We often find great wisdom in the fathers of the church, from Augustine to Thomas Aquinas, to Calvin, Pascal, and on into our own times. They typically are aware of sin from God's perspective, in a way quite foreign to us. Augustine's *Confessions* abound with admission of his own corruption. He describes himself as bound to his passions, incapable of pulling himself out of the mire of his evil habits. But he always does so in the light of God's glory, God's patience, God's gifts, and God's infinite grace. What grieves Augustine is ultimately God's own grief at his condition. It is the same for Calvin, who portrays his own sin as blocking the voice of the Holy Spirit: 'There is no worse screen to block out the Spirit than confidence in our own intelligence.' Sin is in one way about 'blocking God' out of our lives. All the great fathers render the same judgment of sin as an affront to God, rather than merely human foible.

One common mistake many of us make is to think that only the highly dramatic, public sins are worthy of opprobrium.

[5] Ibid., 13.

Shootings in elementary schools, the assassination of a President, a drug cartel, these are the 'real' sins, we often think. Our own smaller sins are but indiscretions, moral lapses. Blameworthy, to be sure, but not 'shocking.' Many of us in America can remember the trauma of Watergate. As layer after layer of the sleaze began to be revealed we felt a mixture of nausea at the pollution from high places and intrigue at the unfolding story. During one key moment of exposure, when a report had clearly been identified as a lie, Richard Nixon declared, 'I guess that statement is now inoperative.' This was a typical way of trying to make little of some rather major deceptions.

We have a way of creating hierarchies of evil. Nearly universally, we would condemn the Holocaust as wicked; no qualifiers. Our family had the chance to visit Auschwitz not long ago. Having read extensively into the literature about the death camp, I imagined I would be somewhat prepared for what I was about to see. I was not. Several things overwhelmed me. First, the extent of the place. Unit after unit, block after block, the camp was far more extensive than I had imagined. To have eliminated over one million people it would had to have been. But when we walked around and visited the endless quarters, 'hospitals', interrogation rooms, kitchens, crematoria, the effect was simply harrowing. Second, the term 'inhumanity' seemed woefully inadequate to express the systematic cruelty we sensed, even decades after the actual events. Human hair for sale, the eye glasses, gold from teeth, children's shoes, parading naked people into gas chambers, all this hit us as far more relentlessly malicious than we had ever thought.

Are not most of our sins but peccadilloes in comparison? At one level, of course, some sins are indeed smaller than others. A small lie is nothing as horrendous as putting millions to death because of ethnic prejudice. But let's be careful here. The so-called larger sins are ultimately in the same category as every kind of sin. And the converse is also true. Every kind of sin, even the smaller ones, offend God in the same fundamental way: we declare ourselves better, wiser than he. We can dull our conscience until it thinks big or little, our sins do not really matter. Hannah Arendt famously remarked when she observed Adolph Eichmann, who had sent thousands of Jews to their death in camps like Auschwitz, on the 'banality of evil.' What she meant by that was not that evil itself was banal, but that Eichmann had convinced himself he was simply doing his job. He showed no signs of remorse, nor, particularly, of anti-Semitism. He told the court he was powerless to change certain actions, even if he knew they were wrong.

Most of us have never done anything so horrible as sending thousands to an unjust death. But most of us are capable of talking ourselves into thinking we are innocent, or that we couldn't change anything even if we wanted to. Yet consider how the Scriptures look at our sins. Nothing banal there!

When we curse someone or resent a person in our hearts is that so bad? Our Lord tells us even to say to someone 'you fool' (*raca*) is liable to the hell of fire (Matt. 5:22). How can that be? Because, as he explains, anger against a brother is the equivalent of murder (vv. 21-22). When we refuse to be reconciled with our neighbor, it is tantamount to disturbing the entire moral order, wherein we are commanded to love our neighbor as ourselves (Lev. 19:18; Matt. 19:19; 22:39). Moreover, refusing to love one's neighbor, even if he is an enemy, is to work against the purposes of a loving God who has himself loved his enemies and reconciled them to himself. God in Christ has already reversed the usual morality of revenge, still so prevalent in our hearts and in many societies (Matt. 5:43-48). An apparently small act, such as cursing one's brother, taken in context, is huge. That is why R. C. Sproul likens sin to 'cosmic treason.'

Cheating on an income tax form is miles removed from treating people as animals for the slaughter as was the case of the death camps. Yet, at another level, when we sin we offend our great God, whatever the sin. Apparently smaller sins, such as deceiving our friend or abusing our spouse, are the same 'stuff' as Nazi cruelty. Really? Yes, because the drive to affront our neighbor, however seemingly small, is nevertheless from the same corrupt heart as that of Rudolf Höss, the commandant of Auschwitz. Only most of the time we lack the opportunity and the pressures that drove the Nazis. Ask yourself this question, 'If I could be sure no one was looking, even God, would I...?' Is not the painful answer, yes, I am by nature capable of such cruelty. The only thing restraining me is my sense of decency, my fear of other people's opinions, my desire not to lose face.

Considered altogether, cheating on an income tax form is actually horrendously damaging. First, we offend the God who told us to pay our taxes and render honor to whom honor is due (Rom. 13:7; 1 Pet. 2:17). Proper honor of human offices which God has ordained is an important way to honor God himself. When we transgress here, we are in fact saying to God, you have no place in my life, least of all a place of authority. Second, we threaten the ability of governors to govern. Without proper government a good deal of social cohesion is broken down. Without the necessary funds, legitimate government agencies cannot do their work, whether it be the courts, the police, the environmental groups, or legislators. Refusing to pay taxes amounts to anarchy. Third, we force others to pay more than they should. I used to work in a jazz band in France. Our drummer was rather an anarchist. He always insisted on being paid in cash, so he wouldn't have to declare his income. To which the rest of us said, thanks a lot, you're making us honest stiffs pay more.

The same goes for lust. For many, often males, looking the wrong way at a woman, glancing at a smutty magazine, or clicking onto a porn site seem trivial, harmless. I am not harming anyone. I have not actually stolen someone's wife. I am not paying money for a prostitute. But, again, Jesus likens lust to adultery (Matt. 5:27-28). Just entertaining a possibility in one's heart, without going any further, is a threat to God's moral order and his provision of marriage. Besides, when we stray into pornography unintentionally we are contributing to a large corrupt industry, one which victimizes (especially) women. Sociologists call this *structural evil*.

If these implications are true in the man-ward sins, are they true as well of God-ward sins? Certainly, and all the more. Such apparently small things as knocking on wood, dropping a swearword or catching up on work on the Sabbath, are, in the larger scheme of things, tantamount to idolatry, blasphemy and refusing God's provision for our lives.

The fact is, what look like minor sins are not so minor after all. To be sure, changing a figure on a tax report is not quite the same thing as armed robbery. Nor is looking at a smutty magazine the same thing as actual adultery. But the point is, it's the same stuff. The only reason we are not as bad as we possibly could be is God's own kind restraint. Here is how Jonathan Edwards puts it in his most celebrated sermon, a sermon as easy to caricature as it is to ignore to our peril:

> There is laid in the very nature of carnal men, a foundation for the torments of hell. There are those corrupt principles, in reigning power in them, and in full possession of them, that are seeds of hell fire. These principles are active and powerful, exceeding violent in their nature, and if it were not for the restraining hand of God upon them, they would soon break out, they would flame out after the same manner as the same corruptions, the same enmity does in the hearts of damned souls, and would beget the same torments as they do in them. The souls of the wicked are in scripture compared to the troubled sea (Isaiah 57:20). For the present, God restrains their wickedness by his mighty power, as he does the raging waves of the troubled sea, saying, '*Hitherto shalt thou come, but no further;*' but if God should withdraw that restraining power, it would soon carry all before it. Sin is the ruin and misery of the soul; it is destructive in its nature; and if God should leave it without restraint, there would need nothing else to make the soul

perfectly miserable. The corruption of the heart of man is immoderate and boundless in its fury; and while wicked men live here, it is like fire pent up by God's restraints, whereas if it were let loose, it would set on fire the course of nature; and as the heart is now a sink of sin, so if sin was not restrained, it would immediately turn the soul into a fiery oven, or a furnace of fire and brimstone.[6]

Too strong? Too negative? The great documents from the Reformation confirm the view that potentially we carry within us the seeds of destruction, powerful destruction, whether or not we let them grow into full flourishing. We have a despoiled nature, our heart is diseased, we are a contaminated spring.[7]

A point of clarification. The Christian life is more, far more, than obeying rules and refraining from certain practices. The Christian life may begin with 'do not be conformed to this world,' but it ends in 'be transformed by the renewal of your mind, that by testing you may discern what is the will of God, what is good and acceptable and perfect' (Rom. 12:1–2). We are made free to enjoy God and to enjoy our neighbors and to enjoy the world he has made.

Thus, refusing to call a brother a fool is not all there is to brotherly love. We are encouraged to use words with our brothers and sisters, not curse words, but grace words. Our speech should be 'always gracious, seasoned with salt' (Col. 4:6). Lively, creative, rich vocabulary is a wonderful part of friendship.

The same with being honest about tax reporting. That is not the end of the matter. Thus, fiscal responsibility does not preclude holding strong opinions about corruption in high places, nor the need for Christians to engage in reform. It is

---

[6] Jonathan Edwards, 'Sinner in the Hands of an Angry God,' *Select Sermons*, Christian Classics Ethreal Library [http://www.ccel.org/ccel/edwards/sermons.sinners.html].

[7] The *Formula of Concord* 1.11; the *Second Helvetic Confession* 8, the *Belgic Confession* 15.

not sufficient simply to be frugal and careful about money, obeying all the rules. The biblical worldview on economics is a large and fascinating subject. If we are merely scrupulous about honest reporting, we have only accomplished a small part of our duties. Being joyful and responsible stewards of God's gifts involves far more than avoiding certain sins.

Likewise, refusing to glance lustfully at the opposite sex is not the only path to sexual responsibility. Christians are not ascetics. Various fathers, such as Tertullian, gave the impression that if we only abstained from lust, all would be well. You will not find a general ordinance for prudery in Scripture. The divine author who inspired the Song of Solomon and the stories of Ruth and Esther is not there to lock us into an attitude of pure restraint. Rather, there is great freedom in the area of sexuality. Only not freedom for adultery and adulterous thoughts.

Sadly, though, in all these matters, we rarely have the balance right. We are sinners through and through. But here is the good news. Only such a bleak diagnosis will stand us in the line for any kind of hope. The prophet Jeremiah tells us the heart is deceitful above all things and desperately sick (Jer. 17:9). But the prophet goes on to plead, in the same breath, 'Heal me, O Lord, and I shall be healed; save me, and I shall be saved' (17:14). Our God can overcome the most desperate wickedness in my heart. He can and he has. Indeed, as Ezekiel tells us, he will give me a new heart, changing my heart of stone to a heart of flesh (Ezek. 11:19; 36:26). In Christ, then, we have been made a new creation (2 Cor. 5:17). And while Christian believers must labor under the weight of remaining indwelling sin, they may, and must, ask, every day, 'forgive us our debts.' And our holy, loving God will do just that. He will wipe the slate clean. He will hide his face from our sins and blot out all our iniquities (Ps. 51:9).

What my neighbor owes me

The petition to have our debts forgiven comes with an addendum: as we forgive our debtors. The complete phrase is, 'as we have forgiven our debtors' (Matt. 6:12). We have here a saying that is easily misunderstood. On the surface it appears that if I can only forgive my neighbor, somehow God must forgive me. There are many versions of this view in popular religion. In certain Asian religions, such as Buddhism, when we build up good *karma* we have a certain amount of goodness coming to us. One occasionally even hears Christians say things such as, 'I went to church today and so have built up some credit with the Almighty.' Of course such statements are not only blasphemy but contrary to the message of the gospel, which tells us forgiveness is a free gift, not something we can earn. Jesus cannot be teaching what is contrary to the gospel. What, then is he saying? This: a forgiven person will naturally be a forgiving person. Only when we have fully grasped the enormity of what God has done for us, can we then imitate him in our relations with others. When we do, it is natural to come back to God and ask for the forgiveness of our daily sins.

Put differently, if we continually harbor resentment and cannot find it in our hearts to forgive other people, what does that say about our own relationship with God? Only when we have begun to grasp the deep grievousness of sin, and the excruciating cost to God for the mercy he showers on us, only then will it begin to be natural for us to turn around and forgive our neighbors. After all, compared to what we have done to God, our neighbor's sin against us is small. This point is made with considerable force in the parable of the unforgiving servant (Matt. 18:21-36). The story is triggered by Peter's question to Jesus: how many times do I have to forgive my brother for his sins against me; as many as seven times? To which the Lord answers, no, seventy times seven. That is, every time, without counting. The parable he uses to give a fuller answer is of a king who comes to settle accounts with his servants. One of them could not pay yet, so he pleads for mercy. The king forgives his debt. But then this forgiven servant goes and finds a fellow servant who owed him a small amount. When he couldn't pay, instead of forgiving his smaller debt, he had him put into prison. When the king heard about it he withdrew the forgiveness and put the man into prison until he could pay his entire debt. The moral of the story is, 'So also my heavenly Father will do to every one of you, if you do not forgive your brother from your heart' (v. 35).

The point here is that someone who knows he is forgiven by God, and feels the blessing of it, should have no problem forgiving his neighbor. Any brother's sin against me is minor compared to my own great offence against God. If God can forgive me, what is it to me to have someone offend me?

This connection must be very important, for it is stressed throughout the Gospels. Indeed, right after the *Prayer* is given, in Matthew's version, Jesus elaborates: 'For if you forgive others their trespasses, your heavenly Father will also forgive you, but if you do not forgive others their trespasses, neither will your Father forgive your trespasses' (Matt. 6:14–15). Jesus makes the mechanics of this clear in a slightly different way in Mark's Gospel: 'And whenever you stand praying, forgive, if you have anything against anyone, so that your Father also who is in heaven may forgive you your trespasses' (Mark 11:25). While it may sound on the surface as though our forgiveness of others is a trigger for God's forgiveness of us, the relation is quite different. Forgiven people (by God) in turn become forgiving (of their neighbor), and so, then, the forgiven person may turn around and ask God again to forgive him or her. No one is perfectly forgiving, of course, but still, the principle still stands that forgiven people ought to forgive others, and when they do they prove that they are in the right relationship with their Father, which relationship becomes the basis for pleading his daily forgiveness of them.

Jesus stresses the urgency of being right with our neighbor in a number of places. Often, being right with a neighbor means extending mercy to them. Earlier in the Sermon he puts it this way: 'Blessed are the merciful, for they shall receive mercy'

(Matt. 5:7). Mercy toward others varies according to their need. Is it material or economic? Mercy finds a way to provide. Is it moral or spiritual? Mercy finds a way to encourage or build up. Has there been an offence? Mercy finds a way to forgive. True mercy does not need to be public. Jesus goes on in the Sermon to extol the virtues of a secret religion, one that does not look for human recognition. In fact, the teaching immediately leading up to the *Lord's Prayer* concerns practicing one's righteousness not before people but only before God. Mercy, in the form of giving to the needy should be so secret that even the left hand doesn't know what the right hand is doing, as it were (6:1–4). So it should be about prayer itself (vv. 5–8). Prayer is before God, not before other people.

Once again, this is not a mechanical procedure. As Daniel Bourguet puts it: 'Among the possible sicknesses in (the realm of) mercy... one is very frequent... The 'merciful' person is sick when his gesture is made with a calculation, when he expects that his gift is made in the hopes of getting another one in return; this calculation renders the merciful person mercantile and stake-holding. As soon as we expect something in return we are sick.'[8] Rather, the merciful person has known mercy because he or she stands forgiven in Christ. Therefore more mercy can be obtained. As in all the beatitudes, the ultimate reward is far greater than the human gesture.

Throughout his teaching and example Our Lord stresses the great urgency of being right with our neighbor. Neither is it an option, nor, even less, a luxury. Right after he explains the gravity of sin by calling an insult worthy of hell, in the passage we looked at above, Jesus says, 'So if you are offering your gift at the altar and remember your brother has something against you, leave your gift before the altar and go. First be reconciled to your brother and then come and offer your gift' (Matt. 5:23–24). We most often think it should be the other way

---

[8] Daniel Bourguet, *Les beatitudes*, Lyon: Olivétan, 2007, 75

around. Is not a worship service the most important activity in life? Not, according to the Lord, if we are not right with our neighbor. And he is not talking about our having something against our neighbor but his having something against us.

Reconciliation is one of the most difficult and unnatural endeavors. Disagreements, arguments, resentments, these occur both in individual settings and in groups, even in countries. As I write this, the United States' government is shut down. What that means is that there is no funding for various governmental activities (except for utter necessities such as the armed forces or government-run hospitals). The reason for that is that our two major political parties have not been able to agree on how to handle our debt ceiling, which allows us to borrow when there is not enough money generated by taxes, etc. I imagine by the time this is published we will have moved beyond the impasse. But to listen to our law-makers day after day blame the other person, sometimes slouching into *ad hominem* or personal attacks, is to witness a sad case of irreconciled people. Each side will have to listen better to the other side. Each will have to give up a little in order to keep the union going.

Francis Schaeffer raises the question how we can continue to exhibit Christian unity without compromise, or without succumbing to what we consider the other person's mistakes.[9] He articulates several crucial principles. He condemns any rejoicing over discovering other people's mistakes. He urges us to measure the seriousness of each disagreement and act accordingly. He taught that at times love is costly, requiring suffering loss for the sake of the relationship.[10] He says we should want to solve the problem rather than win. And he calls us at the

---

[9] Francis A. Schaeffer, *The Mark of the Christian*, Downers Grove: InterVarsity Press, 1970, 26ff. I have elaborated on his approach in *Schaeffer on the Christian Life: Counter-Cultural Spirituality*, Wheaton: Crossway, 2013, 152–155.

[10] Pastor Joseph ('Skip') Ryan, in wedding sermons, often says the newlyweds need to have the priority: 'I'd rather be married than right!'

same time to avoid compromise on issues of right and wrong. One rather moving example Schaeffer presents of depending on these principles is from the German church, specifically the Plymouth Brethren, in World War II. When Adolph Hitler required every religious group to register with the state, half of the Brethren complied, the other half did not. Those who registered had a much easier time of things, while those who did not were subject to all kinds of hardships, including, in some cases, deportation. After the war, reconciliation was a great challenge. Both groups met for several days, bared their souls and searched their hearts. At the end, according to one witness, 'We were just one.'

Here is where Jesus' teaching is radical. Not only should we love our friends, but our enemies. Such an idea is so foreign to the Ancient Near East and its culture, that when he pronounced himself on it there must have been wagging heads. Luke records a kind of mini Sermon on the Mount (Luke 6:17–49). He renders a lengthy discourse on loving one's enemies (vv. 27–36). Some of it sounds nearly masochistic: if someone strikes you on one cheek, offer him the other (v. 29). This behavior is so counter-intuitive for us. But the Lord explains, if you love those who love you what good is it. Even sinners do that. This ethic is radical indeed: be kind to others when you know there won't be kindness paid in return. But why? He does not keep us in the dark. It is because this is how God has treated us. If you act this way, 'your reward will be great, and you will be the sons of the Most High, for he is kind to the ungrateful and the evil. Be merciful even as your Father is merciful' (vv. 35–36).

There it is! We can and must act this way because that is exactly how God has acted toward us. If life were a system of rewards, calculated on a sort of investment (I'll pat your back if you'll pat mine), there is no gospel, no good news. For the good news is that what we deserve is not a pat on the back but a shove into the abyss. Instead, God forgives the 'best' people and the 'worst' people, unconditionally. Once we have grasped this gospel, or, better, once it has grasped us, then we can turn to the relatively easy task of forgiving our enemies. Peter makes the connection this way: 'Having purified your souls by your obedience to the truth for a sincere brotherly love, love one another earnestly from a pure heart...' (1 Pet. 1:22). John puts it poignantly: 'We know that we have passed out of death into life, because we love the brothers' (1 John 3:14). And again, 'Beloved, let us love one another, for love is from God, and whoever loves has been born of God and knows God. Anyone who does not love does not know God, because God is love' (4:7–8).

The unforgivable sin?

A few passages in the New Testament tell us the dreadful news that one sin is not forgivable. Called the sin against the Holy Spirit, we learn about it in several different places. The Synoptic Gospels record that Jesus spoke about that particular offense. It is worth citing all three occurrences, as they are slightly different. Matthew records that 'every sin and blasphemy will be forgiven people, but the blasphemy against the Spirit will not be forgiven. And whoever speaks against the Son of Man will be forgiven, but whoever speaks against the Holy Spirit will not be forgiven, either in this age or in the age to come' (Matt. 12:31–32). Parallel to this, but slightly different, is Mark's version: 'Truly, I say to you, all sins will be forgiven the children of man, and whatever blasphemies they utter, but whoever blasphemes against the Holy Spirit never has forgiveness, but is guilty of eternal sin' (Mark 3:28–29). Luke is more succinct: 'And everyone who speaks a word against the Son of Man will be forgiven, but the one who blasphemes against the Holy Spirit will not be forgiven.'

What sin could be so bad that God is unable to forgive it? Put that way, there isn't one. What about blasphemy? Simply put, blasphemy is speaking contemptuously about God. Not only swearing using his name, but railing against him is blasphemy. One could think of an atheist declaring, 'God is not great.'[11] Or of the Norwegian communist skeptic Arnulf Øverland, who gave a speech in 1933 on 'Christianity—The Tenth Plague.' Such blasphemies can be forgiven, according to Our Lord. We may better understand the blasphemy against the Holy Spirit from the context in the Gospels. In Matthew and Mark we have Jesus' exorcizing of a demon, which drew the comment from the Pharisees that Jesus casts out demons by the prince of demons (the devil). After refuting this charge with the simple argument that the devil wouldn't fight against himself, Jesus then says that the blasphemy against the Holy Spirit is unforgivable. It appears this sin is one of a hard heart. When someone is so inflexibly closed that he cannot receive Christ, it is another kind of blasphemy than simply attacking God. In Luke the context is the denial of Christ before men (Luke 12:9). Presumably this is far more than to 'speak a word against the Son of Man' (v. 10), but rather a fundamental denial that Christ can be God. Again, such a denial is more than just refusing to receive Christ. There is also a stubborn inability to be converted.

One of the functions of the Holy Spirit, both in the Old and the New Testaments, is to reveal God, and open people's hearts to him. To resist the Spirit's work is to oppose the very dynamic of faith, the very possibility of salvation. To arrive at a place in one's heart where we are comfortable calling Jesus the devil, we have so hardened ourselves to him as to have precluded any change. Thus, the sin against the holy Spirit is not a particular sin or blasphemy so much as it is a dreadful hardening. To arrive at such a place might take a lifetime. William Barclay describes the difference between the two kinds of sin. The one, he says, is like the notorious criminal Tokichi Ishii's encounter with Jesus through the Gospels. When he did, he realized the

---

[11] The title of a book by Christopher Hitchens, *God Is Not Great: How Religion Poisons Everything*, New York: Twelve/Hachette, 2007.

horror of his sins. He was 'stabbed in the heart,' convicted of sin because of Jesus' love and beauty. The other, though, is to become completely unable to experience such conviction:

> But, if a man has got himself into such a state, by repeated refusals to listen to the promptings of the Holy Spirit, that he cannot see anything lovely in Jesus at all, then the sight of Jesus will not give him any sense of sin; because he has no sense of sin he cannot be penitent, and because he is not penitent he cannot be forgiven.[12]

Note the emphasis on the *state* of a person, rather than any series of words or actions.

The book of Hebrews describes the kinds of persons who have 'once been enlightened, who have tasted the heavenly gift, and have shared in the Holy Spirit...' who then fall away. At this point, says the author, it is impossible for such a person to be restored again to repentance, for he has, in effect, crucified the Son of God again (Heb. 6:4–8). This is admittedly a difficult passage. What it cannot mean is that there is a category of sin that cannot be forgiven or repented of. Nor can it mean we don't get a second, a third, a fourth chance. What it does mean is that if someone is expecting one further step in the history of redemption, one more episode to come, beside the revelation of Jesus Christ, it is not going to happen. After Christ there is no second chance for another entry point. Such a person may well have tasted the real presence of a heavenly gift, even the power of the age to come, but if he or she expects yet one more chance, a further revelation, it won't happen. 'In these days,' says the author, in contrast to the many times and ways God spoke before, he has spoken through his Son, period, full stop (1:1–2). Jesus is the final installment, the 'yes and amen of all the promises of God' (2 Cor. 1:20). To hope for a next step, and

---

[12] William Barclay, *The Gospel of Mark*, rev. ed., Philadelphia: Westminster Press, 1975, 80–81.

then a next, and a next, is to be of such a mindset that cannot be converted. The passage explains that such a view holds God up to contempt. It compares the person to a land that cannot be cultivated (Heb. 6:6–8). What is scary, of course, is that such a person has already been blessed by the real power of the coming kingdom, and yet does not really belong to it.

John also mentions a sin that cannot be forgiven. He tells us that God will forgive sins 'not leading to death,' and that we should pray for any kind of sin, except the one that does lead to death (1 John 5:16–17). He tells us that there is sin that does not lead to death, which must be prayed for (v. 17). John rather assumes that his readers know what he is talking about. Perhaps the tradition was passed down from the apostles who knew the Gospels' accounts of the blasphemy against the Holy Spirit. Surely, in one sense, all sins are 'unto death.' Paul tells us that the wages of sin is death (Rom. 6:23). He is thinking about all sin, any sin. But here, in 1 John, a special kind of sin is being singled-out, a sin so wicked, we should not even pray about it. We have a clue about what that sin is from the rest of this letter, when the author is discussing sin and righteousness in relation to knowing God. He tells us that everyone who knows God and hopes in him will be purifying himself (3:3). By contrast, by the practice of sin a person shows himself to be of the devil (3:4–10). By 'the practice of sin,' John cannot mean just sinning, since he earlier dealt with us as sinners who are less than honest if we say we are not (1:10). He means something more committed, a way of life, that is sin-bound. Such a pattern, when confirmed, is by definition not forgivable, since the hardened heart cannot, or will not, ask for mercy.

Nathaniel Hawthorne, the nineteenth-century American author, famous for *The Scarlet Letter*, wrote a short story called *Ethan Brand*. The setting is a lime kiln on Mount Greylock, in New England. Ethan used to take care of that kiln. But now he was on a quest. Having begun life as a good and kind man, he began to lust after a special kind of knowledge. He wanted to find the unpardonable sin. In the process he hurt people, ruined a young woman, was rude to a wandering Jew. He finally jumped into the lime kiln. The last bit of the story has the present kiln keeper peering down and seeing his ashes, and a heart of pure limestone. The story is capable of several interpretations, but the main point is that various sins can be forgiven, but if someone is on a quest for the unpardonable sin, he is carrying it about inside. The heart can no longer respond. Such a person cannot be forgiven, nor can he forgive others.

Christ's heavenly high priesthood

The good news, however, is that Christian believers cannot fall prey to the unpardonable sin. The reason is not first and foremost that we have soft hearts or that we are now capable of resisting sin. The reason is that the same Christ who died and was raised for our salvation, is not finished his work, but ever lives at God's right hand in order to intercede for us (Rom. 8:34). Indeed, he 'ever lives to make intercession' for all who draw near to him (Heb. 7:25). Jesus is our heavenly high priest. Unlike earthly priests who need to sacrifice for their own sins, Jesus is 'holy, innocent, unstained, separated from sinners, and exalted above the heavens,' and thus fully able to plead our cause (Heb. 7:26–27). Jesus is like a lawyer who always wins his case (1 John 2:1). The reason he always wins is that his sacrifice was perfect, fully able to propitiate for our sins (v. 2). That word 'propitiation' refers to the removal of God's wrath because of our sin (Rom. 3:24f.). Christ's once-for-all sacrifice succeeded in turning away the wrath of the Father from us, because he received it upon himself.

Few teachings could be more comforting that this one. The Christian faith is the only religion whose God carries the scars from his wounds. When we ask 'forgive us our debts,' we can be utterly sure that God listens. He must listen and answer or deny the work of his Son. The assurance of faith varies from person to person and from circumstance to circumstance. All the great Christian teachers have told about occasions when assurance has diminished. They may have traversed the dark night of the soul, feeling little of the presence of God. Such a valley of the shadow of death may be caused by many things, from falling into sin, to a great loss, or a physical assault such as illness. Yet even here, it is comforting to know that our circumstances change nothing of the heavenly high priesthood of Jesus Christ, nor can they remove one iota from our communion with the Lord. There is no double jeopardy. If God has justified us, then no one can condemn us (Rom. 8:33–34).

We may feel guilty, often justifiably so. But we are no longer truly guilty before the God who has justified us. We may lose our sense of fellowship with the Lord because we have fallen into sin. But it is not the loss of salvation. If God is displeased with us because we have sinned, it is the displeasure of the Father for his children. They ever remain his children regardless of what happens. So, then, when we are in this place, whatever it is we have done, we may say with complete confidence, 'forgive us our debts as we forgive our debtors.' And immediately, we are forgiven. We are cleansed and free!

Prayer

Almighty and most merciful Father; We have erred, and strayed from thy ways like lost sheep. We have followed too much the devices and desires of our own hearts. We have offended against thy holy laws. We have left undone those things which we ought to have done; And we have done those things which we ought not to have done; And there is no health in us. But thou, O Lord, have mercy upon us, miserable offenders. Spare thou them, O God, who confess their faults. Restore thou those who are penitent; According to thy promises declared unto mankind in Christ Jesus our Lord. And grant, O most merciful Father, for his sake; That we may hereafter live a godly, righteous, and sober life, To the glory of thy holy Name. *Amen.* (Book of Common Prayer, 1662)

God, be merciful to me, a sinner! (Luke 18:13)

8

Lead Us not into Temptation
but Deliver Us from Evil

Through many dangers, toils and snares
We have already come
'T was grace that brought us safe thus far
And grace will lead us home (*Amazing Grace*)

Trials

Our English word 'temptation' does not convey the full meaning of the Greek word *peirasmos*, which really means 'test' or 'trial.' Often the word is used in the New Testament to mean the trial of a person's faith or integrity. Peter tells his readers not to be surprised at the fiery trial which comes to *test* them. Instead welcome the affliction because it means we are sharing in Christ's sufferings (1 Pet. 4:12–13). And the ultimate end of withstanding affliction is eternal life. 'Blessed is the man who remains steadfast under trial,' James tells us, 'for when he has stood the test he will receive the crown of life, which God has promised to those who love him' (James 1:12).

Of course, imbedded in every trial are temptations. Hardships, trials, often bring with them the temptation to choose the easy way out. Paul reminds the Galatians that his infirmity (whatever it may have been) was a *trial* to them, yet, he said, they received him as they would an angel from heaven (Gal. 4:14). We do not fully know what Paul's infirmity was. Some argue for a disease. The most likely answer is that he had been so badly afflicted by his persecutors that he came to the Galatians exhausted and beaten up, as we might put it. As such they were tempted to despise him and give no heed to his message. Adversity was often regarded as a divine judgment, a sign of shame. But to their credit the Galatians welcomed him.

When we pray 'Lead us not into temptation,' we are saying, 'do not put us to the test.' We are asking our gracious and benevolent God to spare us the kinds of trials that would bring with them an enticement to fall. The sources for temptation are various. They can come from outward circumstances. Jesus tells his disciples about the seed of the word falling on the rock, and having no root, people will believe it for a while, but then 'in the time of *testing* fall away' (Luke 8:13). Life is hard. Difficulties of all kinds beset us: financial, physical, the burden of work. As I write these pages, a dreadful typhoon has hit the Philippines leaving a wake of devastation and wreckage. Some five thousand people have died and over four million have been displaced. Riveted to the news, we heard extraordinary testimonies of faith despite what might have been a great pressure to abandon belief in a good God.

Temptations embedded in trials can come from inward circumstances, such as one's mental state. Among the most common is greed or covetousness. Paul warns Timothy of the dangers of wanting more than the basics: 'But those who desire to be rich fall into temptation, into a snare, into many senseless and harmful desires that plunge people into ruin and destruction' (1 Tim. 6:9). We remember the story of Faust, who was promised power and wealth, but in the end lost his soul.

The mysterious attraction we have for things, when unbridled, will lead to destruction. John Bunyan gives an amusing if sobering account of such greed in the section in *Pilgrim's Progress* about three characters named Mr Hold-the-world, Mr Money-love, and Mr Save-all! They had all gone to school where their master was Mr Gripe-man in a place called Love-gain, a market town in the County of Coveting in the north. 'This School-master taught them the Art of Getting, either by violence, cousenage, flattery, lying, or by putting on a guise of Religion; and these four Gentlemen had attained much of the Art of their Master, so that they could each of them have kept such a School themselves.'[1] Interesting that the author would have included the 'guise of religion' in his set of tactics for covetously acquiring things.

But deliver us from evil

Often, in the Old Testament, the one who prays asks God for protection against his enemies. And that can still be appropriate. Consider the case of the importunate widow mentioned earlier in this book (Luke 18:1–8). Her 'prayer' was for justice against her adversary. Or, consider the souls under the altar in Revelation 6:9–11, who ask, 'O sovereign Lord, holy and true, how long before you will judge and avenge our blood on those who dwell on earth?' Notice, however, that the *Lord's Prayer* asks more generally for deliverance from *evil*. There are two possible sources for evil, one coming from our own sinfulness, and the other from various afflictions, including illness, natural disasters and enemies. We need to be delivered from both.

An important question is before us. Since we are asking God to keep us from trials and deliver us from evil, where do trials and evils come from? Does God send us trials and dark Providences? If so, does that make him a tempter? Strictly

[1] John Bunyan, *Pilgrim's Progress*, 547.

speaking, the answer to the second question is a resolute no! The very idea that God would tempt someone is an affront to his character. James, again, explains: 'Let no one say when he is tempted, 'I am being tempted by God,' for God cannot be tempted with evil, and he himself tempts no one' (James 1:13). God is pure light. As we saw earlier, he is holy ('hallowed be thy name'), and thus incapable of any malice. What does cause temptation? James goes on to explain, 'But each person is tempted when he is lured and enticed by his own desire. Then desire when it has conceived gives birth to sin, and sin when it is fully grown brings forth death' (James 1:14–15). James here uses imagery from fishing as well as from reproduction. To catch fish one needs a lure or some kind of bait. The birthing process is one of a slow but inexorable development beginning at conception and moving on to birth. Writing in a pagan environment where people believed that they were pawns of supernatural forces, James' words had a sting to them: we, not supernatural forces, and certainly not God, are solely responsible for our foibles.[2]

Evil desires lie in our breast. We are born with them (Ps. 51:5) and we nurture our immoral desires as we advance through the different stages of life. Our hearts, as John Calvin reminded us, are idol factories.[3] Not all human desires are evil, of course. God did not make us stoic, passionless creatures. Hunger for food, the instinct for worship, sexual desire, longing for eternal life, all of these are good, when directed toward the right object. But when marshaled into the service of our selfish pleasure then these desires become evil.

Theologians describe our accountability as 'free agency.' That is, we are free in a fundamental sense. First, because our agency is real. We are not living in a dream world where we

---

[2] See Dan G. McCartney, *James*, Baker Exegetical Commentary on the New Testament, Grand Rapids: Baker Academic, 2009, 106–107.

[3] John Calvin, *Institutes of the Christian Religion*, 1.1.11.

only think we may make decisions. God has created this world with significance, and our decisions are genuine, they make a difference. So much so that our decisions are worthy of blame or approbation.[4] We cannot say, when we sin, 'the devil made me do it,' nor, especially, 'God led me to do it.' One of the oldest diversionary tactics is *blame shifting*. It was first practiced by Adam and Eve after their disobedience. Adam dared say to the Lord, 'The woman whom you gave to be with me, she gave me the fruit of the tree and I ate it' (Gen. 3:12). It was bad enough for him to say that she had given it to him and he ate, as though he had no power to resist. But far worse, Adam explained that this woman (notice she is now a woman, not his beloved wife, Eve) was a gift from God. The implication is clear: God is somehow the real cause of his transgression. We should recoil against this sort of reasoning with everything in our souls. Naturally, God was not fooled, but turned around and put the curse of death on humanity and on the earth where we dwell.

Even in a fallen world, one which is now tainted with evil in every aspect, we do not altogether lose our free agency. Our wills have been damaged, as Calvin puts it, but not annihilated. Though we are now inclined to do wrong, we are still free because we choose to follow our inclination. It is important to explain that there is some mystery to choice-making. Choice is not simply a trigger we can pull. Choice results from our entire dispositional complex. Thus, we may have tendencies, pre-dispositions, not to speak of backgrounds, families, culture, and so much that contributes to who we are. People who grow up in families that struggle with alcohol are more likely to struggle with it themselves than others. People growing up in countries with a long history of oppression or violence may be less prone to be peace-makers. Psychological problems such as depression

---

[4] The essence of free agency is not *libertarian free choice*, which means the ability to go one way or the other, but responsible free agency, which means our decisions are ours, not made for us by any outside force.

or uncontrollable anger may be inherited. Even being tired can weaken us in the face of temptations (Matt. 26:41). Still, even taken into account all these aggravating factors, none of them contradicts either human freedom or human responsibility.

We might ask, as well, what about those of us who are believers, 'born again to a living hope through the resurrection of Jesus Christ from the dead'? (1 Pet. 1:3) What about indwelling sin in Christians? The answer is that we have conflict within us. The conflict is serious, in fact Paul calls it a war (Rom. 7:23; see Gal. 5:16–18). The latter part of Romans 7 describes the power of sin still present in the believer. Paul in effect says we have two 'personalities,' one that loves the law of God and the other, the 'flesh,' which attempts to make us captive to 'the law of sin.' One part of us desires to do the right, the other part is the evil that we persist in doing (vv. 13–23). He calls himself a wretched man, and cries out for deliverance from 'this body of death' (v. 24). He then thanks God through Jesus Christ, and moves on to the magnificent chapter 8, which comforts us in our sinfulness and in our suffering.

So how does this dual personality affect our free agency? If even without regeneration we still had freedom, we have it that much more as believers, because of the two 'personalities'. The most fundamental one, the one which will have ultimate victory through Christ, is the one that delights in the law of God in our inmost being (v. 21). 'For sin,' Paul had told us earlier, 'will have no dominion over you, since you are not under law but under grace' (Rom 6:14). In the new heaven and earth, when we will not be able to sin, we will still be free, more free than ever.

Thus, when we ask God to protect us from trials and deliver us from evil, we are in part asking him to deliver us from our own sinful selves. The previous petition asked him to forgive our sins. We may be forgiven, justified before a holy God if only we ask in faith. But this petition concentrates more on sanctification, the transformation of the sinner into a person more conformed to the image of Christ.

Our chief adversary

Now, to make things more complex, besides ordinary outside forces, and besides being ourselves the source of temptation to sin, we can also be tempted by invisible, demonic forces. The Bible typically names three great adversaries: the world, the flesh and the devil. The flesh, we have already dealt with. The world is that society, that corrupt system which seeks to replace the Lordship of Christ in our lives (Rom. 12:2). Transformation by God's Holy Spirit is the ultimate remedy against worldliness. But so is prayer. As Jacques Ellul puts it, 'If prayer is to be genuine, it presupposes an inward battle against the promptings of the world, which denature the relationship with God, and hence denature God.'[5] While it is we alone who are responsible for yielding to temptation, and thus we are the fundamental tempting agents, yet outside temptations from the world exist and are sometimes very enticing. 'Evil is a sucker for solidity,' said exiled Russian poet Joseph Brodsky. 'It always goes for big numbers, for confident granite, for ideological purity, for drilled armies and balanced sheets.'[6]

Many times, then, the tempters are other people. Our Lord was particularly severe in condemning anyone who might lead a child into sin. Better for that tempter to be drowned in the sea! In a cryptic statement, Jesus then adds, 'Woe to the world for temptations to sin! For it is necessary that temptations come, but woe to the one by whom the temptation comes' (Matt. 18:6-7). We might think of some of the infamous cult leaders or the great dictators of modern times. They often have powers of persuasion which can galvanize crowds and individuals to follow them and to commit heinous crimes. Through the New Testament we are told to be vigilant against any human tempters who would prey on God's people (Acts 20:29-31; 2 Tim. 3:1-9; 1 John 4:1).

---

[5] *Prayer and Modern Man*, op. cit., 145.

[6] 'A Commencement Address,' *Less Than One: Selected Essays*, New York: Farrar, Straus & Giroux, 1986, 385.

However, our chief opponent in life is Satan. He is sometimes called the tempter, though he has other names (Matt. 4:7; 1 Thess. 3:5). When David took a census of his people for his self-aggrandizement, he is said to have been incited by Satan, Israel's enemy (1 Chron. 21:1). Satan entered Judas, who would betray Jesus to his adversaries (John 13:21). He 'filled' Ananias who lied about his gift to the early church (Acts 5:3). He tempts unmarried people to illicit sex (1 Cor. 7:5). Those fallen from the church are said to have 'strayed after Satan' (1 Tim. 5:15).

We rightly ask what kind of power this dark figure possesses that he can command such authority over people? Satan undoubtedly holds a position of considerable power. In Job 1:6 he is numbered with 'the sons of God,' a reference either to angels or to pagan royalty. Like the angels, he has access to the presence of God, a privilege which will be removed from him in the end (Rev. 12:9). Even the angel Michael found him to be such a redoubtable opponent he could not curse him directly, but invoked the name of God to challenge him (Jude 9). Satan directs a vast organization committed to the destruction of God's people (Matt. 25:41; John 12:21; Eph. 2:2; Rev. 12:7). 'The greed and self-centered ambitions of the nations, the deceptive diplomacy of the political world, the bitter hatred and rivalry in the sphere of commerce, the godless ideologies of the masses of humanity—all springs out of and are fostered by satanic influence.'[7]

The New Testament gives various accounts of demonic oppression and even possession (Matt. 8:16–17, 28; 12:22; Luke 8:2; 13:11, 16; Mark 5:4; 9:25, etc.) A question can be raised about the exact relation between a demon's destructive work and disease, including mental illness. For example, the account of the boy healed by Jesus in Matthew 17:14–18 identifies him as 'epileptic' (*selezianomai* in Greek can mean 'moon-struck,'

---

[7] D. E. Hiebert, 'Satan,' *The Zondervan Encyclopedia of the Bible*, vol. 5, Grand Rapids: Zondervan, 2009, 334.

because the ancients—though surely not Matthew—believed certain seizures were intensified during the increase in the moon's light). At the same time the account tells us that Jesus cast a demon out of him, and he was instantly healed. In another account, a 'mute and deaf spirit' is cast out of a young lad (Mark 9:25). Without being categorical, it is safe to say that demon-possession was real, particularly in the time of Jesus' ministry, when one would expect fierce opposition to his work. At the same time there must often be a relation between certain types of demon possession and illness. Medical science today, itself a great gift of God, is able to look into the biological nature of any number of illnesses and propose treatments of various kinds. While we cannot rule out the possibility of a demon's involvement in some cases, it is not wise to try to duplicate the work of exorcism as it is displayed in the New Testament. Nowhere are we encouraged to exercise such a 'gift.' Rather, we are enjoined to pray and administer oil, no doubt the 'oil of gladness' foretold in Isaiah 61:3 (James 5:14). It should go without saying that we also would want the sick to visit a medical expert, already a practice in the New Testament (Matt. 9:12; Luke 5:31, Mark 2:17; Col. 4:14).

Are we to conclude from these facts that Satan is so powerful that to face him is hopeless? Not at all. First, Satan is limited. He may be a perverted angelic figure, but he is a creature. His power is limited by God's permission. When he came from roaming on the earth to ask God if he could test Job's faith, God allowed him to harm Job, even to send tragedy Job's way, but to leave him alive (Job 1:12; 2:6). His power has been 'delivered' to him (Luke 4:6).

Second, Satan is defeated. While God may at times even use Satan to discipline his wandering people, Satan can never bring them down (John 10:28; Rom. 8:38-39; 1 John 4:4). The Gospels record a telling incident. After casting out a demon, some of Jesus' critics quipped, 'He casts out demons by Beelzebul, the prince of demons' (Matt. 12:24; Luke 11:15; see

Mark 3:22). The charge is very serious, for it implies that Jesus is something like a sorcerer. Such an attitude is what can lead to the sin against the Holy Spirit, discussed earlier. Jesus' reply is as powerful as it is logical: 'Every kingdom divided against itself is laid waste, and no city or house divided against itself will stand. And if Satan casts out Satan, he is divided against himself. How then will his kingdom stand?' (Matt. 12:25–26). He goes on to explain, 'But if it is by the Spirit of God that I cast out demons, then the kingdom of God has come upon you' (v. 28). He adds, if you want to plunder a rich man's house, you must first tie-up the rich man (v. 29). There is a good deal going on here. But at the least our Lord is pointing out that Satan's house is being plundered, because he is being bound by the power of the Holy Spirit.

> Satan is defeated! Indeed, as Luther's great hymn puts it,
>> And though this world with devils filled
>>> should threaten to undo us,
>> We will not fear,
>>> for God hath willed His truth to triumph through us:
>> The prince of darkness grim, we tremble not for him;
>> His rage we can endure, for lo, his doom is sure,
>>> One little word shall fell him.

That 'little word' is of course the Word of God, particularly the gospel. He is powerless before the Word of God, so we should not hesitate to use it.

The last Adam

How can we be so sure? Because Jesus Christ has already conquered Satan. He has disarmed him. Not only has he plundered his house and tied him up in the process, but he continues to usher-in the kingdom over against the devil's self-proclaimed rights. Throughout Jesus' earthly life, and then upon his death, the devil pursued him with the goal of undoing him in his messianic purposes. One of the most dramatic occasions was at the very beginning of his public ministry. After his ordination (the baptism by John), the Spirit led him into the wilderness where he fasted for forty days. Jesus was in a weakened state, we might say a vulnerable state (Luke 4:1-13; cf. Matt. 4:1-11; Mark 1:12-13). Satan's basic purpose in these temptations was to thwart Jesus' ministry by offering him short cuts. He first suggested he turn some stones into bread. Jesus was hungry, the temptation was real. The more so in that the devil said to him, 'If you are the Son of God,' then make these stones become bread. Jesus' response was swift and decisive: 'It is written, "Man shall not live by bread alone"' (v. 4). The second temptation was the offer to give Jesus all the kingdoms of the world, if only he would bow down and worship him. There was a half-truth in what Satan said: 'To you I will give all this authority and their glory, for it has been delivered to me, and I will give it to whom I will' (v. 6). In a certain sense Satan had been given (the Greek word here means 'committed' or 'permitted to have') the kingdoms of the world. And to make this temptation the more alluring, Jesus had come to win the kingdoms back from Satan's power. But, again, the answer is swift and decisive: 'It is written, "You shall worship the Lord your God, and him only shall you serve"' (v. 8)

The third temptation is a bit different. Satan somehow brings Jesus to the pinnacle of the temple and then tells him to jump off, because Psalm 9:11-12 predicts that angels will keep him and protect him from injury. We presume Jesus was brought to the southwestern corner of the Herodian temple, a high point with a great valley below. It is not entirely certain why the devil chose this place. One natural possibility is that Jesus being rescued by angels would be in the full view of many people. Another is that Satan knew that the temple had special significance because it would be destroyed, and the worship of Jesus, the true temple would replace the building (John 2:18-22). Or it could be that Satan was following Daniel's prophecy about the cruel tyrant Anthiochus Epiphanies forcing the Jews to worship pagan gods in their very temple (The 'abomination of desolation' Dan. 11:31; 12:11). If Jesus obeyed his suggestion then he could proclaim his power to trump such an outrage. In any case, Satan was surely tempting Jesus to fulfill Scripture but in a perverted way. Having quoted Scripture twice to refute him, the devil may have said to himself, I can do that as well, and proceeds to quote Psalm 9. But once again, Jesus counters him with an authentic use of the Bible: 'It is said, you shall not put the Lord your God to the test' (v. 12). Then we are told the devil ended *every* temptation (were there more?) and departed from him *until an opportune time* (v. 13). He would be back!

We might say that the three temptations recorded in Luke represent three enticements to achieve something good, but delivered in a wrong-headed way. It's a case where the ends do not justify the means. What are the ends? First, the social calling to feed the hungry. Jesus came to do just that. At the least, his miracles of the multiplication of the loaves and fishes attest to this desire on his part (Matt. 14:17ff.). But not on Satan's terms. 'Man shall not live by bread alone,' as we saw earlier, is not about absolutes, but about relatives. Jesus would feed the hungry, but first as the 'bread of life' (John 6:35), who provides food of the right kind for our deepest hunger. This same provider will indeed ultimately remedy world poverty, and asks us to enlist in the task with him. Second, the political goal. We need to rid the world of oppressors. Jesus was bent on doing such a work. But not by bowing to Satan who is the greatest oppressor of all. Jesus would indeed reclaim all the kingdoms of the world, but by the power of his resurrection, not an obsequious bow to the pretender (Col. 1:15-20). And, finally, indeed, the Scriptures are all about Jesus Christ coming and demonstrating his great power (Luke 24:25-27). But not in a raw demonstration of supernatural magic. Rather, in the painstaking, thorough work of reconciling people to God (2 Cor. 5:18-19). Certainly, Jesus will come again in his full power as judge, but in this present time of God's patience, he works by saving the lost and bringing them under the true and loving authority of the Lord God.

Notice that to face Satan Jesus does not use special, supernatural weaponry. He arms himself with the same artillery as must we who are his followers: the Word of God. This 'one little word' which can fell Satan is still our best weapon, and highly effective. Notice as well that Jesus quotes entirely from the Book of Deuteronomy (8:3; 6:13; and 6:16). While he could have quoted from other portions of Scripture, this particular book has special relevance. It was written to prepare God's people to enter the Promised Land after an entire generation had perished in the wilderness because of their rebellion. So, where Israel had failed, Jesus succeeded. Indeed, his test, and all of his trials, are similar, yet more difficult, to those of Israel. He was hungry. He was directly confronted by Satan. His temptations were issued in rapid succession.

Jesus, indeed is the last Adam, the second man (1 Cor. 15:45-7). Inasmuch as Adam failed the test to decline the fruit of the forbidden tree, leading humanity in his train, Jesus, whose life and death were an act of obedience, leads the new humanity into eternal life. And in so doing he brings justification and life to believers, a far greater legacy than we can imagine (Rom. 5:12-21). Because of Jesus' obedience to the Father, 'The God of peace will soon crush Satan under your feet' (Rom. 16:20).

In practical terms, then we can avoid two extremes, and find a third way. The one extreme is to ignore the power of Satan. French poet Charles Baudelaire once quipped, 'The great ruse of the devil is to persuade you he doesn't exist.' Having said all we have about his power and stratagems, we ignore him at our peril. The other extreme, though, is to exaggerate his power, or even to nurture an unhealthy fascination in Satan and his minions. Various ministries exist which teach that behind every human problem there is a demon. I once heard an evangelist describe the demon of nicotine, the demon of calories, and so forth. No, Satan is a conquered enemy. Though he still prowls around, 'Resist him, firm in your faith' (1 Pet. 5:9). Or, as James tells us: 'Submit yourselves therefore to God. Resist the devil and he will flee from you' (James 4:7).

God's part

So, then, if these are our real enemies, and if God cannot in any sense be said to tempt us, is he altogether absent from our trials? Of course, not. Here we enter into a world of apparent contradictions. But they are only apparent. Because we find Bible texts which affirm with the greatest authority that God ordains whatsoever comes to pass. 'Our God is in the heavens; he does what he pleases' (Ps. 115:3). 'Whatever the Lord pleases he does, in heaven and on earth, in the seas and all depths' (Ps. 135:6). God 'works all things according to the counsel of his will' (Eph. 1:11). He ordains large things, such as historical events (Acts 17:26). The king's heart is in his hand (Prov. 21:1). So are human actions (Prov. 16:9; Jer. 10:23). But God also attends to the smallest things such as birds who feed (Matt. 6:26). Here is how Joni Eareckson and Steve Estes put it:

> All during these sins, typhoons, illnesses, mishaps, snake bites, crib deaths, famines and gas-station robberies— *God hasn't taken his hand off the wheel for thirty seconds.* His plans are being accomplished despite, yes, even through, these tragedies. They *are* tragedies. He considers them so. He loathes the wickedness and misery and destruction itself—but he had determined to steer what he hates, to accomplish what he loves.[8]

Somehow God ordains things but yet hates them! God's ordination must include trials and evil itself. He turns the heart of the Egyptians to hate his own people and deal wickedly with

[8] Joni Eareckson Tada & Steve Estes, *When God Weeps: Why Our Sufferings Matter to the Almighty*, Grand Rapids: Zondervan, 1997, 69.

them (Ps. 105:25). In one of the most astonishing statements in Scripture, we are told that 'I [the Lord] form light and create darkness, I make well-being and create calamity, I am the Lord, who does these things' (Isa. 45:7). The Hebrew word for 'create' is *bara'*, the same word used in Genesis 1:1 for the creation of the heavens and the earth in the beginning. God hardens hearts (Rom. 9:18). And it gets even stronger. He commanded a 'lying spirit' to entice Ahab's prophets (1 Kings 22:21–23). God sends those who are perishing a 'strong delusion, so that they may believe what is false...' (2 Thess. 2:11).

Now, lest we think the Bible is teaching some sort of Islamic determinism, we need to throw up a few cautions. For one, as we have seen, the Bible affirms with great authority that God is neither accountable for evil nor can we blame him for its existence. The Thessalonians passage goes on to assert that those deceived ones will be condemned because they refused to believe the truth and instead enjoyed unrighteousness (2 Thess. 2:12). We often find that the two affirmations, God's ordaining and human responsibility, are put alongside one another without raising a problem. The book of Exodus records the series of episodes whereby Pharaoh's heart is hardened against the people of Israel (Ex. 4–11). We are told several times that God hardened his heart. Nearly as frequently are we told that Pharaoh hardened his own heart. Peter tells the audience at Pentecost that Jesus was 'delivered up according to the definite plan and foreknowledge of God,' and then adds that 'you crucified and killed [him] by the hands of lawless men' (Acts 2:23).

We might try to ask a question to which there is no answer, at least, no humanly acceptable answer. If God ordains whatsoever comes to pass, then why did he create a world in which evil would be introduced? We do not know. We can safely say, for his own glory, but that does not get us very far. Several times, when people begin to ask such a question, they are referred to God's utterly different ways from our own. After Job's nearly intolerable suffering, and after he had asked, several times, why he could not find God in order to set forth his case for the unfairness of his trials, the Lord finally answers him out of the whirlwind: 'Who is this that darkens counsel by words without knowledge?' (Job 23:1–9; 38:1ff.). One might have thought God owed Job an explanation. But no. Not that there isn't one, but it is not accessible to him or to us. Describing the unbelief of his own people, Paul explains that God has mercy upon whom he has mercy and hardens who he wills (Rom. 9:18). When the rhetorical question is asked, why then does he find fault, since no one can resist his will, Paul does not detain them in a long philosophical discussion of 'compatibilism,' the idea of the ultimate harmony between divine sovereignty and human free agency. Instead, he says, 'But who are you, O man, to answer back to God?' (vv. 19–20).

Having said that there is ultimate mystery, we do not have to end all discussion there. Many of the texts in Scripture about God's sovereignty over evil are not addressing the hard philosophical question of why he would allow it in the first place. They are saying that once evil enters into the world, by the fault of human beings, then God will use it, even it, for his own good purposes. There are scores of examples. One of the best-known is Joseph's remark to his brothers. After having sold him into slavery and caused him excruciating pain and anguish, through a remarkable set of Providences Joseph became the ruler of all Egypt, second only to the Pharaoh himself. Because of his prophecy about years of plenty followed by years of want, Pharaoh put him in position to sell food to those who came to Egypt for it. As he was able to distribute food to people all over the world, including his own guilty brothers, he was able to tell them, 'As for you, you meant evil against me, but God meant it for good, to bring it about that many people should be kept alive, as they are today' (Gen. 50:20).

Final victory

What is absolutely certain, then, is that whenever God sends a dark Providence into the lives of his people, it is for their greater good. Suffering produces endurance, Paul tells us. And endurance issues in character, which in turn produces a hope that cannot shame us, but rather will put into mind that God is lavished upon us through his Holy Spirit (Rom. 5:3–5). So great is this reality that is should cause us to rejoice even in our sufferings. Notice carefully that we are not told that suffering is good, nor that somehow the greater the pain the greater the gain. Such masochistic notions have no part in Scripture. But a certain kind of suffering, sent by God into our lives, refines our faith, as we saw in our introduction on prayer (James 1:2–4; 1 Pet. 1:7). If we suffer for the sake of righteousness then we are blessed (1 Pet. 3:13).

Not only is our faith refined through suffering, but we are in close fellowship with Christ, who suffered for our sins (1 Pet. 3:18). There is mystery here, but when we suffer, we somehow participate in the sufferings of Christ. Paul tells the Philippians that he is privileged to share in Christ's sufferings, 'becoming like him in his death, that by any means possible [he] may attain the resurrection from the dead' (Phil. 3:10–11). Astonishingly, he tells the Colossians that in his sufferings for their sake, '[he is] filling up what is lacking in Christ's afflictions for the sake of his body, that is, the church' (Col. 1:24). Such thoughts must be handled with care, lest we imagine that somehow Christ's sufferings were not sufficient for our redemption. Such a thought is preposterous. The entire New Testament rings clear, that when Jesus died, as he himself said it, 'it is finished' (John 19:30). In contrast to the Old Testament priest, who had to perform a yearly sacrifice, Jesus Christ did not suffer repeatedly, but 'appeared once for all at the end of the ages to put away sin.' He was 'offered once, to bear the sins of many' (Heb. 9:23–28).

What is meant by filling up the suffering that remains is not suffering for atonement of sins, but the suffering that Jesus in heaven continues to experience for the sake of his people. He told the unconverted Saul on the road to Damascus that he was persecuting him, and causing pain like the ox driver who prods his beast (Acts 9:4–5; 26:14). Our Lord is not a passionless phantom. He hurts when his people hurt.

Suffering and trials are not to be desired. 'Put us not to the test,' our petition exclaims. 'Lord, please let this cup be taken away,' Our Lord himself asked in the Garden, as we have seen. God does not enjoy sending trials to his people. We rightly ask him to spare us hardship. Yet there are times when the hardship will come. And so we then ask, 'deliver us from evil.'[9]

No people group has reflected on this more profoundly than African Americans. During their unspeakable suffering in slavery, they sang about Jesus on Calvary. They asked Jesus to walk with them. One of the most thoughtful gospel songs is 'Lord Don't Move That Mountain.' When we have prayed, 'lead us not into temptation' and the trial stands before us intact, if that mountain will not be removed, then we may pray:

> Now Lord don't move my mountain
> But give me the strength to climb
> And Lord, don't take away my stumbling blocks
> But lead me all around

If the mountain cannot not be removed then the Lord will give us the strength to climb it. If the mountain will not be removed then the Lord will show us a way around it.

Paul told the Corinthians that trial would come. But he adds that no trial comes upon us that is not common to humanity. Yet with each trial, he will also provide the way to endure it, and then the way to escape it (1 Cor. 10:13). What a marvelous thought. Whatever our trials, however hard, with the eyes of

---

[9] The Greek could be translated, 'deliver us from the evil one,' meaning Satan. But for various reasons the more generic term *evil* is to be preferred.

faith we will find a way to endure and a way out. The ultimate way out, of course, is death, which in now 'swallowed up in victory,' and takes us to complete victory. We may have trouble imagining that when we suffer we are in such fellowship with humanity, and especially with Jesus. If so, we must ask for more faith, and also benefit from people who have been through such trials and have been the stronger for it.

Don Carson, in his book, *How Long, O Lord?* has a section titled, 'Things Worse Than Death.'[10] He tells about being diagnosed with a rare disease. The prognosis for those afflicted varies from mild to lethal. Fortunately, it turned out that his was the mild variety. But during the months he reflected on the prospect of his own death. He decided that the hardest part of dying would be leaving his wife and children. He determined that if the news were bad he would do everything he could to prepare his family. Besides that, he could not think of a reason why death would be such a bad thing. He then modestly tells the reader that he did not come to this place after prolonged meditation on the glories of living with Christ. He knew with Paul, however, that 'to live is Christ and to die is gain,' so that to depart would be much better, yet he had wished these realities could grip him more persistently. And so should we all.

Prayers

Lord, You know what is best; let this be done or that be done as You please. Give what You will, as much as You will, when You will. Do with me as You know best, as will most please You, and will be for Your greater honor. Place me where You will and deal with me freely in all things. I am in Your hand; turn me about whichever way You will. Behold, I am Your servant, ready to obey in all things. Not for myself do I desire to live, but for You - would that I could do this worthily and perfectly!

(Thomas à Kempis, *The Imitation of Christ*, 1427).

[10] D. A. Carson, *How Long, O Lord?* Grand Rapids: Baker, 1990, 119–120.

When the storm of life is raging
    Stand by me
When the storm of life is raging
    Stand by me
When the world is tossing me
Like a ship upon the sea
Thou who rulest wind and water
    Stand by me.

In the midst of tribulation
    Stand by me
In the midst of tribulation
    Stand by me
When the hosts of hell assail
And my strength begins to fail
Thou who never lost a battle
    Stand by me.

In the midst of faults and failures
    Stand by me
In the midst of faults and failures
    Stand by me
When I do the best I can
And my friends misunderstand
Thou who knowest all about me
    Stand by me.

When I'm growing old and feeble
    Stand by me
When I'm growing old and feeble
    Stand by me
When my life becomes a burden
And I'm nearing chilly Jordan
O Thou 'Lily of the Valley'
    Stand by me

(Charles A. Tindley, *Spiritual*, 1906)

9

For Thine Is the Kingdom
and the Power and the Glory
Forever and Ever, Amen

> The doxology with which, following the older versions, we
> round off the Lord's Prayer is not in the best manuscripts.
> Nevertheless, it is the best tradition! (J. I. Packer)

Paeans of praise

A *doxology* is an act of praise to God. Most of us are familiar
with 'The Doxology.' When we are invited to sing it, we tend to
know it by heart.

> Praise God from whom all blessings flow
> Praise him all creatures here below
> Praise him above ye heavenly hosts
> Praise Father, Son and Holy Ghost. *Amen.*

This Doxology was written in 1674 by Thomas Ken, a minister
in the Church of England. Originally it was the final verse of
two longer hymns: 'Awake My Soul, and With the Sun,' and

'Glory to Thee, my God, this Night,' used in morning and evening prayers, respectively. The doxology is most commonly sung to the tune, Old 100th, written by Louis Bourgeois for the French Protestant Psalter.[1]

Many of us are also familiar with the *Gloria Patri*, a Trinitarian doxology which also has an ancient pedigree. The version often sung in Protestant churches is this:

> Glory be to the Father, and to the Son, and to the Holy Ghost,
> As it was in the beginning, is now and ever shall be,
> World without end, Amen, Amen.

The formula, 'world without end,' is a modernization of the biblical formula that establishes the praise of God forever (Gal. 1:5; Phil 4:20, etc.).

Doxologies are found throughout the Bible. The apostle Paul often ends his letters, or even a significant section of a letter, with outbursts of thanksgiving. He concludes his letter to the Philippians (just before final verses with greetings and a blessing) with, 'To our God and Father be glory forever and ever' (Phil. 4:20). The same is true of 2 Timothy: 'To him be the glory forever and ever, Amen' (4:18). A more elaborate farewell doxology is found in Romans 16:25–27. Occasionally, as when speaking about the power of the gospel, he calls out, praising God (Gal. 1:5; Eph. 3:20–21; 1 Tim. 1:17).

After a long and involved defense of God's good plan in view of the present disaffection of Israel, a plan involving divine election, the grafting-in of the Gentiles, God's impartiality toward those who have faith in Christ, whether Jew of Gentile, Paul is nearly speechless. He can only exclaim,

[1] Bourgeois (1510–1560) wrote it for *Pseaumes Octante Trois de David* (1551), which was the second edition of the Genevan Psalter. He wrote it originally as the setting for Psalm 134. William Kethe paraphrased Psalm 100: 'All People that on Earth Do Dwell' and used the Bourgeois melody, hence the name Old 100th. Kethe was a Scot, presumably one of the Marian exiles, and published this and other Psalms for singing in the Anglo-Genevan Psalter of 1561.

> O the depth of the riches and wisdom and knowledge
> of God! How unsearchable are his judgments and how
> inscrutable are his ways... for from him and through him
> and to him are all things. To him be the glory forever.
> Amen (Rom. 11:33).

For other writers it is the same (Heb. 13:21; 1 Pet. 4:11; 5:11; 2 Pet. 3:18; Jude 25). As might be expected, the Book of Revelation is overflowing with doxologies (1:5–5; 4:11; 5:13; 7:12). And, of course, the Old Testament is replete with blessings and expressions of thanks to God.[2]

True enough, we neither find the doxology in Luke's version of the *Lord's Prayer* nor in the earliest manuscripts of Matthew's. The first known use of the doxology, a shorter version, is in the *Didache*, the late first century 'teaching' which represented the early church's concern to train new members into the ethics and sacraments of the Christian community.[3] Significantly, the words of the doxology that conclude the *Lord's Prayer* are nearly identical with David's blessing in the great assembly in preparation for the construction of Solomon's great temple:

> Blessed are you, O Lord, the God of Israel our father,
> forever and ever. Yours, O Lord, is the greatness and the
> power and the glory and the victory and the majesty, for all
> that is in the heavens and in the earth is yours. Yours is the
> kingdom, O Lord, and you are exalted as king above all...
> (1 Chron. 29:10–11).

We find a similar doxology sung after the *Lord's Prayer* in the *Divine Liturgy* of the Byzantine Catholic or Greek Catholic Churches.

For our purposes we may celebrate this doxology as a most appropriate conclusion to the *Lord's Prayer*, even though it is

---

[2] For a helpful summary of doxologies with an analysis of their function, see [http://cranfordville.com/DoxologiesInTheNT.pdf] .

[3] *Didache* 8.2.

not found literally as the appendix of the versions in Luke or Matthew. If only because we find doxologies throughout the Scripture, particularly David's blessing, it seems right to say it and have it guide us.

The kingdom and the power

Having prayed that God's kingdom would come and his will would be done on earth as it is in heaven, we now can declare that the kingdom and the power are his. His rule is *not yet* fully extensive, yet it is *already* his: 'Thine is the kingdom.' Such a truth needs constantly to be reaffirmed.

Nebuchadnezzar had built up his magnificent kingdom, founded on the glories of his own person. Babylon, under his rule, was as luxuriant as it was powerful. He ruled with ruthless purpose. He constantly refused the warnings and calls to repentance issued though God's servant Daniel. Daniel had pleaded with him to break off from his sins and show mercy to the oppressed, a counsel to which he was deaf (Dan. 4:30). Then, in the full glory of his reign, everything changed. He was smitten by a disease that made him mad. His symptoms indicate that he was afflicted with lycanthropy, a rare condition in which the victim thinks himself to be an animal (the Greek word *lukos* means 'wolf'). Accordingly he fled people, and lived in the fields, eating grass like oxen, his hair and nails long (Dan. 4:32). After seven years he would be restored and confess that only the Lord God rules over men.

What a picture of God's sovereignty in contrast to human pretension. No matter how powerful the earthly ruler might be for a while, a godless kingdom will always fail. Whether it be the Pharaohs of Egypt, Alexander the Great, the Roman Emperors, Louis XIV the 'Sun King,' the ruthless Napoleon, the modern dictators, or any other potentate, big or small, their reign will be brought to nothing. This occurs not only because such realms inevitably self-destruct, but because God in his great authority will not allow human pretenders to rival his rightful rule. Just before Nebuchadnezzar's demise, he had a dream in which his humiliation was predicted. He was told, 'The sentence is by decree of the watchers, the decision by the word of the holy ones, to the end that the living may know that the Most High rules the kingdom of men and gives it to whom he will and sets over it the lowliest of men' (Dan. 4:17, cf. v. 32).[4]

Throughout the Scripture we learn that our God reigns. 'The Lord has established his throne in the heavens, and his kingdom rules over all' (Ps. 103:19). The Bible is replete with affirmations of God's great power. 'I am the Lord your God, who stirs up the sea so that its waves roar—the Lord of hosts is his name' (Isa. 51:15). Mary, echoing the doxology of Hannah, praises God because 'He had brought down the mighty from their thrones and exalted those of humble estate' (Luke 1:51).

Jesus himself became the supreme ruler of the universe after his resurrection. Already all things, including thrones and dominions, were created through him. But now, as the firstborn from the dead, he is preeminent in everything (Col. 1:15–20). To what end, such power? Of course, the nations are judged. The Book of Revelation reminds us constantly of the judgments poured out on the world because Christ had opened up the seal of history (Rev. 5:5). But also, this great power is being used today to bring thousands of people to the gospel. The church can preach the gospel of discipleship to all the nations because all authority in heaven and on earth has been given to him (Matt. 28:16–20).

Not everyone is moved by the sounds of baroque music. But few settings of doxologies match Georg Friedrich Handel's 'Worthy Is the Lamb' from *Messiah*, a setting of Revelation 5:12 from the ancient translation.

---

[4] Watchers and holy ones are pagan figures from Babylonian religion, but here playing the role of angels in the divine council. Daniel interprets this dream as coming from the true God.

> Worthy is the Lamb that was slain to receive power,
> and riches, and wisdom, and strength,
> and honour, and glory, and blessing.
> Blessing, and honour, glory and power,
> be unto Him that sitteth upon the throne,
> and unto the Lamb for ever and ever.
> Amen.

The opening section, 'Worthy...' is slower and meditative. Then comes the successive affirmations of God's power and riches... Finally, a wonderful fugal 'Amen' that stretches out over many measures, reaching a climax with full orchestra, loud trumpets and pounding timpani!

And the glory forever, Amen

Glory is a word we often use casually. We speak of a glorious meal, a glorious sunset. This is proper, of course. But the primary way Scripture uses the word is connected with the dazzling splendor of authority. Thus, the most glorious person of all is the Lord God. God's glory is often portrayed as a great light, the *shekinah*, as later Judaism would name it. This great light shone in the tabernacle and the temple (Ex. 40:34; 1 Kings 8:10-11). God has become a beautiful diadem for his people (Isa. 28:5). God is said to dwell in the beauty of holiness (1 Chron. 16:29; Ps. 29:2).

To pray, 'thine is... the glory' is to declare what is the greatest ultimate. God's name is itself glorious. Thus, it is good and proper to 'fear his glorious name' (Deut. 28:58). But it is also right to thank him and praise his glorious name (1 Chron. 29:13; Neh. 9:5). The central problem of humanity is that it lives to praise its own name and revel in its own glory. Paul explains to the Romans that the reason everything has gone wrong in the world is because people have refused to honor and thank the God who can clearly be discerned both in the world outside and in the conscience inside (Rom. 1:21, 25). And yet the very purpose of human existence is to glorify God.

The glory of God is certainly manifest in the things he has made, and in the splendor of his presence. But the apex of his glory is in the humiliation and exaltation of Jesus Christ. When the Second Person became a man, the *shekinah* was hidden, and yet the disciples testified, 'we have seen his glory, glory as of the only Son from the Father, full of grace and truth' (John 1:14). Beside the unique moment when Jesus appeared on the mount of transfiguration next to Moses and Elijah, where his face shone as the sun and his clothes were white as light, there was something to Jesus' teaching and authority that truly was glorious (Matt. 17:1–8). Most especially, Jesus was glorified when he was 'lifted up' on Calvary's cross, and then raised up from the dead (John 17:5). Because of his extraordinary humiliation, God 'has highly exalted him and bestowed on him the name that is above every name' (Phil. 2:9).

For that reason, 'every knee should bow, in heaven and on earth and under the earth, and every tongue confess that Jesus Christ is Lord, to the glory of God the Father' (vv.10–11). We thus begin now what we shall be doing in all eternity, lost in wonder, love and praise, Amen! That little word means, 'so be it,' 'I agree,' 'it is true.'

A transforming vision

The *Lord's Prayer* is indeed a transforming vision. Not only is it a worldview, that *sees* the world right side up. But it is a prayer, thus a way of life that brings *transformation*. Praying it sincerely will sanctify us, will renovate us, will make us people better able to glorify, but also to enjoy God forever.

Prayer is hard. It does not come naturally to fallen creatures. It is a discipline to be practiced, and yet it must guard against the rote heaping up of empty phrases, lest its very purpose be compromised. When we struggle with the reality of prayer, our prayer may simply be, 'Lord teach me to pray, so that I will more clearly see your face.' He will, because he has already. He has taught us this special prayer. And then, we wait for the Lord. He will come to us in his own good time. How do we know? Because that's the gospel! Jesus became man, prayed all his life, was crucified, died and was buried, and then was raised up on the third day, so that the very power we lack may be proffered on us. When we cry to him out of the depths, and we wait upon him like watchmen for the morning, the morning will come, and we will know his steadfast love, his full redemption from all our iniquities (Ps. 130).

Prayers

Bring us, O Lord God, at our last awakening into the house and gate of heaven to enter into that gate and dwell in that house, where there shall be no darkness nor dazzling, but one equal light; no noise nor silence, but one equal music; no fears nor hopes, but one equal possession; no ends nor beginnings, but one equal eternity; in the habitations of thy glory and dominion, world without end, *Amen*. (John Donne, 1572–1631)

Praise the Lord, all nations!
  Extol him, all peoples!
For great is his steadfast love toward us,
  And the faithfulness of the Lord endures forever.
Praise the Lord!

(Ps. 17)